T0170229

Scaling the Heights

SCALING THE HEIGHTS

Thought Leadership, Liberal Values and the History of The Mont Pelerin Society

EAMONN BUTLER

Institute of
Economic Affairs

First published in Great Britain in 2022 by
The Institute of Economic Affairs
2 Lord North Street
Westminster
London SW1P 3LB
in association with London Publishing Partnership Ltd
www.londonpublishingpartnership.co.uk

The mission of the Institute of Economic Affairs is to improve understanding of the fundamental institutions of a free society by analysing and expounding the role of markets in solving economic and social problems.

A CIP catalogue record for this book is available from the British Library.

ISBN 978-0-255-36818-6

Many IEA publications are translated into languages other than English or are reprinted. Permission to translate or to reprint should be sought from the Director General at the address above.

Typeset in Kepler by T&T Productions Ltd
www.tandtproductions.com

Printed and bound by Page Bros

CONTENTS

ABOUT THE AUTHOR

Eamonn Butler is Director of the Adam Smith Institute, one of the world's leading policy think tanks. He holds degrees in economics and psychology, a PhD in philosophy and an honorary DLitt. In the 1970s he worked in Washington for the US House of Representatives, and taught philosophy at Hillsdale College, Michigan, before returning to the UK to co-found the Adam Smith Institute. He has won the Freedom Medal of Freedoms Foundation at Valley Forge and the UK National Free Enterprise Award; his film *Secrets of the Magna Carta* won an award at the Anthem Film Festival; and his book *Foundations of a Free Society* won the Fisher Prize.

Eamonn's other books include introductions to the pioneering economists Adam Smith, Milton Friedman, F. A. Hayek and Ludwig von Mises. He has also published primers on classical liberalism, public choice, capitalism, democracy, trade, the Austrian School of Economics and great liberal thinkers, as well as *The Condensed Wealth of Nations* and *The Best Book on the Market*. He is co-author of *Forty Centuries of Wage and Price Controls*, and of a series of books on IQ. He is a frequent contributor to print, broadcast and online media.

ACKNOWLEDGEMENTS

The Society and I are very grateful to the family of our late friend Max Hartwell for their permission to borrow heavily from his work. I also thank Bruce Caldwell and Alberto Mingardi, my successor as Secretary of the Society, for their helpful comments and criticisms.

PREFACE

In 1995 the Liberty Fund published *A History of the Mont Pelerin Society*, written by the Oxford historian (and past President of the Society) Professor Max Hartwell. The book provides a very full account of the Society's first half century, but is now difficult to obtain and much has happened since 1995.

With that in mind, in 2012 the Board of the Society asked me, as the incoming Secretary, to précis Hartwell's *History* and bring it up to date. It was hoped that this would give members, prospective members and other scholars a digestible short guide to the history and ethos of the Society and to some of the key individuals and events that have shaped it.

Ten years later, on the Society's 75th anniversary, the Board have asked me to update the text yet again.

1   WHAT IS THE MONT PELERIN SOCIETY?

Max Hartwell opens his *History* by saying that the Mont Pelerin Society is 'not well known' and has 'no demonstrably proven role in world affairs'. This remains true. But while the Society itself remains little known among the public, many of its individual members are indeed both well known and influential in the academy and in world affairs.

Some, for example, have been government ministers (e.g. Sir Geoffrey Howe in the UK, Antonio Martino in Italy, Ruth Richardson in New Zealand and George Shultz in the US) or senior officials (such as former Federal Reserve Chairman Arthur Burns and Polish National Bank Chairman Leszek Balcerowicz). A few have been presidents or prime ministers (among them Ludwig Erhard of Germany, Luigi Einaudi of Italy, Mart Laar of Estonia, Ranil Wickremesinghe of Sri Lanka and Václav Klaus of the Czech Republic). Several have influenced economics and culture sufficiently to win a Pulitzer Prize (Felix Morley and Walter Lippmann) or a Nobel Prize (including Friedrich Hayek, Milton Friedman, James M. Buchanan, Gary S. Becker and Mario Vargas Llosa). Others, including educators, journalists, businesspeople and leaders of policy think tanks across the world, have wielded influence in different ways.

Yet they have done all this as individuals, not as representatives of the Mont Pelerin Society. The Society's sole contribution to world affairs is its provision of a forum for debate, discussion, study and self-education among its members, their guests at meetings and young scholars – not through political action. It has no official views, formulates no policies, publishes no manifestos, aligns itself with no party and accepts no political or public funding. It does not even try to reach agreement on anything. No votes are taken. Instead, it promotes free and frank debate, aided by a long-standing policy that its discussions are neither broadcast nor reported (though some of the set-piece lectures and presentations are now recorded and appear online).

The battle of ideas

The Mont Pelerin Society was created as a response to the social, political, intellectual and moral ruin that had gripped Europe before and during World War II. The aim of its founding members was modest: to keep alight the intellectual flame of liberalism (the word is used in the European sense) during the dark post-war days and to critique the centralising interventionist notions that then prevailed. The original members, writes Hartwell, 'shared a common sense of crisis – a conviction that freedom was being threatened and that something should be done about it'. That threat, they concluded, was the result of erroneous theories about history, society and economics. As for doing something, they committed themselves not to political action, but to winning the intellectual battle of ideas.

The Society has played a crucial role in that battle. It has done more than just keep liberal ideas alive; it has expanded and deepened liberal philosophy and spread liberal thought across the globe. Equally profound, and even more subtle, has been the strength, courage, friendship, learning and ideas that members draw from and provide to each other. And as members of the Society, liberals who may otherwise feel intellectually isolated and overwhelmed can take strength from the realisation that they are not alone in their approach to social issues.

The Mont Pelerin Society achieves all this, even though it exists 'mainly in the minds and affections of its members,' as Hartwell neatly puts it. The Society has no offices or endowment. Its work is done by a Board of elected, unsalaried members from many countries, with only part-time paid administrative support – usually provided by the Treasurer's own private office. The large international conferences that it holds all over the world are proposed, organised and financed, not by the Board, but by local volunteer members.

Strength through diversity

The Society exists for the mutual education, support and benefit of its members. It is a loose association of people who believe in the power of ideas to change the world for the better. They support the idea of a free society – even if they disagree profoundly on exactly what that means or how it can be achieved. The Society's founder, the Austrian-born British economist, political philosopher and (later) Nobel laureate, Friedrich Hayek, saw it as 'a kind of international academy' for discussing and diffusing liberal ideas. Not an academy in the sense of being confined to college teachers and students, but in the sense of a meeting place for thoughtful people seeking intellectual debate and self-education on matters of importance.

Over the years there have been arguments – almost to the point of destruction, as we shall see – about how activist the Society should become. Yet it has never endorsed the calls to be more political and has remained true to its founding aim of bringing together individuals who wish to defend, support and develop a functional and robust liberal philosophy.

That liberal philosophy inevitably covers a wide range of views and opinions. Members of the Society have very different conceptions of a liberal society: some would call themselves classical liberals, some neoliberals, others anarcho-capitalists, and many other descriptions besides. Their approaches to solving social and economic problems can be very different too; for example, members include methodological individualists, neo-classical marginalists, empiricists and various others. And they debate a wide variety of issues, such as the appropriate role and size of the state, the theory of government, the history of liberal ideas, economic intervention, and monetary policy (always good for an argument between monetarists, 'gold bugs', Austrian School economists and, more recently, nominal-GDP targeters).

While there is 'general agreement about the kind of liberal economic and political order that would promote stability and freedom,' says Hartwell, it remains 'difficult to spell out the details of such an order that would have the approval of all members'. That is certainly true; but it is a measure of the Society's intellectual fecundity, not a mark of its failure.

MPS Nobelist No. 1 (1974) Friedrich A. Hayek (1899–1992)

The Society's founder, F. A. Hayek, was one of the most intellectually fertile liberal thinkers, writing on economics, political science, psychology and the history of ideas. With Ludwig von Mises, he developed the Austrian School explanation of boom–bust cycles, attributing them to unsustainable cheap credit stimulus policies. He became professionally famous as the main intellectual critic of John Maynard Keynes in the 1930s, and popularly famous for his 1944 book *The Road to Serfdom*, explaining how easily social democracy could slide into totalitarianism. His 1960 book *The Constitution of Liberty* traced the development of classical liberal thought and sought to apply it to modern problems.

Hayek's key insight was the concept of *spontaneous order*. Institutions such as markets and the price mechanism are orderly, he observed. But nobody designed those orders nor the behavioural rules that produced them: they evolved because they worked. That evolution required individuals be free to act on the dispersed information available to them. Spontaneous orders could be highly complex, and able to process far more information than any single mind could grasp; it was folly to suppose we could safely replace them with 'rational' planned alternatives. Instead, a liberal government would limit itself to creating the conditions, such as the rule of law, for functioning social orders to emerge.

2 THE PREHISTORY OF THE SOCIETY

The twentieth century was characterised by the politicisation of life: bigger government covering a more extensive range of public issues; political decisions replacing private responsibilities; central planning; and the erosion of long-held freedoms.

The century also brought wild economic fluctuations, stagflation, dictatorship and two destructive world wars. To liberal thinkers, such as members of the Mont Pelerin Society, these outcomes are no mere coincidence.

The expansion of the state

The debate about the proper size of government and its effects on society goes back centuries; but the seeds of the great twentieth-century expansion of government were sown in the nineteenth. Capitalism was criticised as failing the poor. Breakthroughs in science and engineering led social reformers to believe that social and economic life could be engineered just as effectively, and that the scourge of poverty could be eliminated through rational public policy. Welfare states were created, and governments took on much broader functions – including education, healthcare, housing, transport, utilities and industrial production – all of which expanded and grew. By 1926, the influential Cambridge economist John Maynard Keynes could write the epitaph of the free economy, *The End of Laissez-Faire*.

The strongly prevailing view in 1920s and 1930s Europe, in particular, was that 'rational' government intervention was both desirable and inevitable. Few people saw any connection between the expansion of economic and social planning and the erosion of fundamental freedoms.

But liberals did, actively critiquing the collectivism of the time – with some intellectual success but with very little impact on the public and political mood. While the critiques were important, liberals concluded that they needed a more positive approach. They needed to construct a new and more modern version of classical liberalism. They sought to build a liberal narrative for the times: perhaps what the German economist Alexander Rüstow would call *neoliberalism* to distinguish it from the old classical liberalism and laissez-faire approach of the eighteenth and nineteenth centuries. (Later, the Italian economist and statesman Luigi Einaudi would argue that all liberal thinking was 'neoliberalism' because it took timeless principles but applied them to current challenges.)

The Colloque Walter Lippmann

To further this effort, the French philosopher Louis Rougier organised a colloquium of 26 prominent intellectuals in Paris in 1938. It was named the Colloque Walter Lippmann after the American journalist and author of the 1937 book *An Enquiry into the Principles of the Good Society.*

Several of the participants later become founders of the Mont Pelerin Society: Friedrich Hayek, Ludwig von Mises, Michael Polanyi and Wilhelm Röpke. (Another of the Society's founders, Walter Eucken, was invited to the conference but the German regime refused him permission to travel.)

The group established the International Committee for the Renewal of Liberalism, and a second meeting was held in January 1939. But the onset of World War II, just a few months later, stifled those plans. Nevertheless, the colloquium provided Hayek with a useful model for a similar liberal revival after the hostilities had ended.

Hayek's proposal

When the London School of Economics was evacuated from London during the war, Keynes found Hayek rooms at King's College, Cambridge. It was here that Hayek wrote *The Road to Serfdom*, published in 1944. The book explained how even well-intentioned attempts to redesign society could ultimately lead to the extinction of human freedom itself.

Of course, the Nazi regime could hardly be accused of being well intentioned. Germany in the 1930s had been a dismal example of life without liberty, which then elided into the horrors of war and genocide. Hayek saw this as not just a matter of historical chance, but a process of cause and effect. *The Road to Serfdom* was his analysis of how such a process would be likely to play out. Given the world's experience of those times, the huge success of the book in both Europe and America seems no surprise.

And yet, as the war was moving towards its end, talk of the need for *more* state planning and control resumed, with even greater vigour. Hayek knew that countering this stubborn orthodoxy was both urgent and vital, and he was already working on a way to do it.

At a January 1944 meeting in King's College, chaired by the economic historian Sir John Clapham, Hayek discussed whether Europe's liberal civilisation could ever be restored after the war. The next few years would be critical, he argued. Germany and others would need to rediscover the intellectual and moral values on which European civilisation had originally been built – values such as the sanctity of truth, the fundamental importance of individual freedom, the role of democracy and 'opposition to all forms of totalitarianism, whether it be from the Right or from the Left'. To aid that rebirth, Hayek suggested creating an international society 'half-way between a scholarly institution and a political society', along with a journal dedicated to debating these principles.

The organisational challenge

An international initiative on the scale Hayek had in mind would be costly. But others were thinking on parallel lines. In 1945 the German-born political economist Wilhelm Röpke (later a leading architect of Germany's post-war social market economy), who also feared the 'mortal threat' of collectivism to Europe's cultural inheritance, circulated a 'plan for an international periodical' to tackle the problem. He asked Hayek and other intellectuals to contribute and, with the help of Swiss businessman Albert Hunold, began raising money for the venture.

In the event, Röpke raised much less than he needed; but his efforts had revealed the existence of a critical mass of liberal scholars in Europe, and in the US too. Hunold suggested that the money already raised could be used to finance Hayek's idea for a meeting.

Hayek believed that a strong American participation was vital – though the travel costs at that time were daunting. Fortunately, doors were opened by the huge popularity of *The Road to Serfdom* in America and the success of Hayek's lecture tour there to promote it. The William Volker Charities Fund agreed to meet the costs of the American participants, while Hunold secured finance for the Europeans. At last the meeting that Hayek had proposed almost three years earlier could go ahead.

MPS Nobelist No. 2 (1976) Milton Friedman (1912–2006)

Friedman was a prominent critic of the Keynesian orthodoxy that governments could manage inflation, boost employment and achieve economic growth through their taxing and spending policies. He argued that only restraining the quantity of money in circulation could control inflation and provide the basis for employment and growth; but money was a very blunt instrument, and governments should give up their 'fine-tuning' micro-management efforts.

His work on economic and other policy issues convinced him that government action was generally counterproductive. Rent controls, for example, reduced the quality and supply of rental accommodation; licensing requirements for professions such as law, accounting and medicine reduced competition and benefited the practitioners more than the public; and minimum wages made it harder for inexperienced, poor or minority workers to get jobs.

His book (written with his wife Rose) *Capitalism and Freedom* (1962) on these themes turned him from an academic economist into a famous public intellectual. It addressed problems such as educational standards, discrimination, monopoly and poverty, and proposed radical solutions, including flat taxes, privatisation and decriminalising drugs. His regular *Newsweek* columns (1966–84) made him one of America's most famous policy commentators.

Friedman's TV series *Free to Choose* (1980), again co-written with Rose, brought his arguments for free markets, open trade, freedom and capitalism to people (and policymakers) around the world.

3 THE FOUNDING OF THE SOCIETY

'Hayek's arguments for the formation of the Mont Pelerin Society were both intellectual and practical,' writes Hartwell. Intellectually, he believed that a new version of liberalism had to be written, one that could be applied to the social problems of the day instead of just leaving the argument to the interventionists.

The practical challenge

In practical terms, Hayek knew that the talents of isolated liberals had to be brought together, as the Colloque Walter Lippmann had done, such that they could combine and reinforce each other more effectively.

In December 1946 – slightly anticipating success on the funding front – Hayek sent invitations to 58 people to attend the meeting. It would take place on 1–10 April 1947, at the Hôtel du Parc in the Swiss mountain village of Mont-Pèlerin (meaning Mt Pilgrim), overlooking Lake Geneva.

It was short notice, and some could not come, including Antony Fisher, the British businessman who became – on Hayek's suggestion – an intellectual entrepreneur, going on to found the Institute of Economic Affairs and the Atlas Economic Research Foundation (now the Atlas Network). But Hayek did not want to delay a task he thought so urgent.

It was indeed a critical time. After two world wars separated by a massive economic depression, people now craved security more than freedom. During World War II, governments had taken direct control of national economies, but by 1947 there were calls to continue that central direction in order to 'win the peace'.

Thirty-nine participants made it to Mont-Pèlerin. They came from ten countries, seventeen of them having made the long journey from America. Most were academics, twenty of them economists. Another eight came from other fields including law, history, political science, chemistry and philosophy. The group also included influential journalists, thoughtful authors from the business world and policy researchers who today we would call think-tankers.

The weighty agenda

The village of Mont-Pèlerin was an ideal retreat for scholars to discuss the issues facing Europe and debate the different liberal answers to them. It was both remote – at the end of a funicular railway up a steep mountainside – and inspiring: Milton Friedman, one of the younger participants, wrote home to his wife (and later co-author) Rose to report that he could not believe the beauty of the place.

There would be plenty of issues for these talented liberals to grapple with during their ten days in a mountain retreat – as Hayek's long agenda confirmed. What were the essential characteristics of a competitive order? What should be done about monetary instability? Should governments regulate monopolies, wages and agriculture? Can governments keep unemployment down? How should non-market 'public' goods be produced and distributed? Is security and solidarity more important than competition and economic growth? Is liberalism a matter of belief, or can its correctness be demonstrated logically? Is a free economy necessary for a free society? How important to liberalism is religion? How far has the appreciation of liberal civilisation been poisoned by the bias of politicised historians? And the stark question of the times: can Germany ever be rehabilitated?

Unity and disagreement

There is no detailed record of this inaugural meeting, though Albert Hunold's notes and many of the papers delivered there still survive. But even though the participants shared a liberal outlook, it would have been remarkable if they had been in complete harmony on these difficult questions.

And disagreements there were: on the state control of monetary policy, for example; on the role of religion; on minimum wages; and on the level of welfare provision that a free economy could bear. Some participants, such as Röpke and the Swiss academic and diplomat William Rappard, believed that classical liberalism had to be tempered by the contemporary human desire for security. Others, such as the Austrian economist Ludwig von Mises, feared that such concessions were the first step down the road to serfdom, and took a more libertarian stance. Indeed, during the session on income distribution, where some participants were expressing support for the idea of progressive income taxes, Mises famously got up and complained: 'You are all a bunch of socialists!'

There was much more agreement on other topics, such as how the writing of history had been used as a weapon of illiberal propaganda; the over-vaunted role and presumed efficacy of government; and on the importance of constitutional values and the rule of law as essential safeguards for liberty. In general, there was far more to unite the participants than divide them. They were, after all, in their different ways, all liberals who felt an urgent need to revitalise the liberal approach and to counter the damaging errors of interventionism and socialism.

Formulating a statement

In his final circular before the conference, Hayek reminded the group of their 'common convictions' and of the necessity of formulating a statement of the 'common principles on which the work of the organization is to be based' – though this should not be any form of 'public manifesto'.

Yet there remained sufficient differences to make such a statement difficult to formulate. A committee of six produced a draft. Freedom, they insisted, was threatened down to its roots by the 'intellectual error' of imagining that there exist inevitable 'laws of historical development' to which moral standards must be given up. Freedom, they argued, could survive only alongside 'an effective competitive market', which in turn required 'a proper legal and institutional framework'. And if state power was not to erode the free society, 'government activity should be limited by the rule of law'.

But the group could not agree on this draft. Perhaps it was too specific, too long and too uncompromising. Lionel Robbins, of the London School of Economics, was asked to rewrite it. His version, agreed and signed by everyone apart from the French economist and physicist Maurice Allais, remains the Society's guiding statement even to this day.

The Statement of Aims

The Statement of Aims begins starkly and warns: 'The central values of civilisation are in danger.' In some countries, it went on, freedom has disappeared entirely; in others it is 'under constant menace'. Even freedom of thought and expression is being curbed. Freedom is being sacrificed to 'a view of history which denies all absolute moral standards' and 'questions the desirability of the rule of law'.

This, it says, requires study on several fronts: explaining the crisis of the time; redefining the functions of the state; reaffirming the rule of law; establishing minimum standards that are compatible with the market; combating the misuse of history; and safeguarding international peace, liberty and trade.

The Statement of Aims concludes by emphasising the intellectual – and not political – purpose of the Society.

'The group does not aspire to conduct propaganda,' it insists. Nor does it seek to define some precise orthodoxy. It is politically unaligned, aiming only to help preserve and improve the free society by 'facilitating the exchange of views among minds inspired by certain ideals and broad conceptions held in common'. Seventy-five years later, that mission remains unchanged.

The choice of name

Another organisational question for the group was what to call itself. Originally, Hayek thought of taking a name from some great liberal thinker. He considered several before alighting on the English historian and statesman Lord Acton (1834–1902), an independent-minded democrat who knew that 'power tends to corrupt' and to whom morality and liberty were supreme values, not something that could be sacrificed to some political end. Hayek then added the name of Alexis de Tocqueville (1805–59), the French statesman and political thinker who wrote of his 'passionate love for liberty, law and respect for rights'. Hayek's suggestion of 'The Acton–Tocqueville Society' would unite the names of these two great liberals.

But the participants at Mont-Pèlerin could not agree. Acton's name did not command general approval; he was too socially conservative for some. Mises pointed out that de Tocqueville had served under Napoleon; the young American economist Milton Friedman thought the group should be named after principles, not individuals. As an alternative, the French philosopher and economist

Bertrand de Jouvenel proposed 'An Academy for the Study of the Philosophy of a Free Society', but Robbins disliked the word 'Academy'.

Eventually the German–American economist Karl Brandt suggested simply naming the group after the place where they were meeting. The Austrian–British philosopher Karl Popper objected that such a name would be meaningless. But since no other name could be agreed, Brandt's suggestion was adopted and, in its anglicised form, the name 'Mont Pelerin Society' is still used today. The 'meaningless' nature of the name actually became a boon: the name does not commit the Society to any particular views and excludes no one.

MPS Nobelist No. 3 (1982) George J. Stigler (1911–91)

Stigler was a microeconomist who brought empirical rigour to the study of prices, regulation and industrial organisation. He also wrote on the history of ideas in neoclassical economics and pioneered the new field of the economics of information.

His book *The Theory of Price* (1946) examined prices, consumer behaviour, production and costs, monopolies and cartels. Using real empirical data, it undermined traditional assumptions based on anecdote and speculation.

The book took Stigler into regulation, the field for which he is best known. He found that electricity price regulation had in fact only a tiny effect on electricity prices. Again, he concluded that economists should study the real workings of regulation, rather than assuming them. While economists assumed that regulation existed to correct market failures, he showed that governments commonly regulated at the call of producers who sought to use regulation, backed by state authority, to promote their own interests, such as thwarting competition. Regulators even become apologists for the industry they regulate – *regulatory capture* – until regulation becomes more damaging for consumers than the original market failure.

Pioneering the economics of information, Stigler's research on the labour market showed him that job seekers need a spell without work to search for a better job. Job seekers are equally information seekers. Stigler concluded that information is much undervalued in the study of economics.

4 EARLY ORGANISATION OF THE SOCIETY

Non-profit incorporation

Within five years of this first meeting, the Society was formally registered in the US as a non-profit corporation, with more than 60 members. Its stated purpose was 'To study and promote the study of political, economic, historical, moral and philosophic aspects of civil society having a bearing upon the institutional and organizational conditions compatible with freedom of thought and action.' It would also 'hold and sponsor meetings' and 'issue reports, announcements and other documents'.

In early 1952 the US authorities confirmed the Society's tax-exempt status, recognising it as 'organized and operated exclusively for education purposes' and intended 'to facilitate an exchange of ideas' on 'the principles and practice of a free society' as well as to 'study the workings, virtues and defects' of market systems.

Early governance

The original Memorandum of Association set up a nine-member Board and a Council comprising the Board members and six others. But as Hartwell reports, 'In practice, the division between the Board and the Council was pointless' because most decisions were made, with the tacit agreement of the others, by Hayek as President and Hunold as European Secretary.

This informal arrangement would cause major problems later on, though, as Hunold came to assume more and more authority, to the consternation of Hayek and many other members.

A committee set up in 1962 to revise the constitution proposed a more businesslike arrangement: to replace the Board and the Council with a single Board of fifteen, comprising a President, Treasurer, Secretary and twelve others, from among whom Vice Presidents would also be chosen. Board members (other than officers) would have a defined tenure and would retire in rotation. These recommendations were adopted at the 1964 meeting in Semmering, Austria.

Organisational issues

There was also much discussion on how to further the aims of the Society. In 1962 the English economist John Jewkes complained that the Society had 'done little or nothing to draw young people into membership', nor had it extended its membership into crucial areas such as Japan, Central America and South America. The national groupings, he went on, were largely inactive. The Society was always short of funds, and the lack of a salaried secretariat meant that a huge amount of administrative work fell onto an unpaid Secretary.

Some of Jewkes's suggestions, such as building up a trust fund and devolving the administration down to national levels, attracted little enthusiasm. Others, such as raising the membership dues and instituting fees for the (previously subsidised) meetings, were adopted – though more from necessity than choice.

The membership issues were addressed more squarely. By the 1968 meeting in Aviemore, Scotland, the Society's membership stood at roughly 350. Of those, 140 came from the US and another 109 from Germany, France and the UK. Other regions of the world were now better represented. Japan had an impressive 21 members, and there were at least a few from India, Brazil, Argentina, Chile, Uruguay and Venezuela.

The obverse of this was that size was now becoming an issue. The reach of the Society and its ideas was expanding, but the intimacy of the original meeting at Mont-Pèlerin was being lost. There were many, often conflicting, proposals on the matter. A working party of members from various countries could not agree on capping membership numbers. But one thing everyone agreed on was that the ad hoc membership arrangements that were tolerable for an informal association of a few dozen members, with sketchy nominations submitted at the last moment on scraps of paper, 'should now be put on a more business-like footing'.

Looking at the demographic profile of the membership, the working party proposed that preference should be given to younger candidates, and to those from countries where the Society was poorly represented. To maintain standards and aid the scrutiny of potential new members, however, it recommended that candidates should not be considered for membership until they had attended at least one meeting as a guest.

The working party also recommended that more philosophers, historians and political scientists should be admitted. Hayek himself had not intended that the Society should devote itself as much to economic questions as it did: at the original 1947 meeting he had expressed regret that the historians and political scientists were far outnumbered by the economists. The feeling that the Society should broaden its membership is one that has frequently resurfaced in the subsequent decades.

The Montreux decisions

In 1971 the size, membership and organisational questions were thrashed out at a Special Meeting of the Board in Montreux, Switzerland, on the shores of the lake below Mont-Pèlerin. On membership, the Board imposed a five-year limit of 25 new members a year. A Recruitment Committee would be set up to screen nominations and to search out prospective members. Membership dues would be doubled (from $10 to $20).

On meetings, the Board agreed that there should be General Meetings every two or three years, with Special or Regional meetings in between. In general, guests would have to be people thought suitable as future members. Guests should pay higher registration fees than members, though members should pay the actual cost of the conferences, without subsidy. Grants would be made to help younger prospective members to attend.

The original constitution agreed at the 1964 General Meeting in Semmering, Austria, as modified by the Montreux decisions, would serve the Society, with only slight further adjustment, for the next 45 years.

Sources of financial support

The Mont Pelerin Society has never had a large endowment, and only rarely has it had any paid administrative help. It flourishes only because of the loyalty of its members, the enormous voluntary effort of its office-bearers and the willingness of local groups to arrange meetings.

Meetings may take two or more years to plan. They involve a huge time commitment from local organisers and are required to be self-financing – very seldom in recent years have meetings been subsidised from central funds. Yet there is no shortage of willing volunteers: the honour of hosting the Society is reckoned to be reward enough.

One enduring expense for any international society, however, is travel, and for this purpose the Society has solicited specific grants from foundations for the travel of officers, speakers and young scholars. The Volker Fund, as mentioned, financed the American participation in the inaugural meeting in 1947, and over the years other generous grants have come from the Reim Foundation, the Earhart Foundation, the Lilly Endowment, the Roe Foundation, the John M. Olin Foundation, the Scaife Family Charitable Trust, the Pierre and Edith Goodrich Foundation, the Garvey Foundation and other foundations, as well as companies and individuals from many countries. Nor should one overlook the in-kind and logistical support that office-bearers rely on from their own companies, think tanks and academic departments.

Despite this, financial strains have sometimes led to tensions within the Society. The most serious was in 1958 when Hunold, who as European Secretary shouldered most of the administrative work, began to complain about the financial burden of it all. Since 1946, he said, his institution had spent around $30,000 (about $300,000 today) and he personally had spent $20,000 (about $200,000 today). He asked to be paid $3,000 a year, financed from higher membership dues and new charges on those attending conferences. Fritz Machlup, as Treasurer, was shocked: he thought charging for meetings would exclude all the academics and leave the Society with only business members.

MPS Nobelist No. 4 (1986) James M. Buchanan (1919–2013)

Buchanan, with his colleague (and fellow Society member) Gordon Tullock, developed Public Choice economics. Their pioneering book *The Calculus of Consent* (1962) used the tools of economics to analyse government decision-making.

While mainstream economists thought that government policy could correct market failure, Buchanan and Tullock argued that self-interest undermines the rationality and efficiency of public decision-making. Election results were the uncertain outcome of a contest between competing and irreconcilable interests. Debates were dominated by lobbyists with strong interests in the outcome. Politicians appease such groups to 'buy' the votes they command. Then to get their measures through the legislature, they indulge in reciprocal vote-sharing – 'logrolling' – which leaves us with more legislation than anyone rationally desires; and the officials who enforce those laws impose their own interests – perhaps by adding complexities to boost the need for their expertise. The policies that emerge from this process may be more damaging than the problem they are meant to solve: as well as *market failure*, there is *government failure* too.

Simple majority voting makes decision-making easy but also makes it easy for majorities to impose their views (and the costs) on minorities. Qualified majorities (say, two-thirds) make decision-making harder, but exploitation harder too. Buchanan therefore explored constitutional and voting arrangements designed to make essential decisions feasible while minimising the exploitative power of majorities.

5 THE EARLY YEARS

Activism or academy?

In the Society's early years there were disagreements about how 'activist' it should be. The first meeting was a great success in terms of stimulating ideas and forging new contacts, but some members wanted to do more than just that.

The divisions surfaced at the first Board meeting of the newly incorporated Society in 1948. Some, such as Brandt, Hunold and the American journalist (and later Pulitzer Prize winner) Felix Morley, considered the threat of collectivism so great that quick practical action was necessary. The French economist and government adviser Jacques Rueff wanted this to include the Society publishing a liberal manifesto directed at influencing public opinion. Others, including the German economist Walter Eucken, the Italian philosopher Carlo Antoni and Hayek himself, wanted the Society to focus on research and study that would fight and win the battle of ideas, discredit socialism and outline the liberal alternative.

This latter view prevailed, though disagreements persisted. Brandt and Rueff continued to press for a more policy-oriented approach. Morley wanted the Society to be more 'aggressive'. The Danish economist Carl Iversen thought that even as a 'scientific' society the Society could still work with policy groups. Leonard Read of the Foundation for Economic Education felt that without a policy role, the Society had little future.

A second conference

Despite these doubts about direction, there was agreement among the Board that a second conference should be held, if only to clarify the group's purpose. Hunold and Brandt, both on the 'activist' wing, raised the funds, and the meeting took place in Seelisberg, Switzerland in 1949. It discussed practical questions such as labour and wage issues, the role of the state in education and the demand for social security: the Society was beginning to fashion its critique of post-war interventionism. But alongside the intellectual agenda, members also debated the aims and future activities of the Society. Brandt wanted an active secretariat, vigorous fundraising, policy groups and publications. However, the majority did not agree.

The discussion resumed at the 1950 meeting in Bloemendaal, Netherlands. Hayek argued, successfully, that the Society should be a 'community of liberal scholars' not a policy group. 'He believed,' writes Hartwell, 'that the Society's competitive advantage lay in ideas, not in action, and that in the long run the influence of the Society would be greater if its efforts were intellectual rather than political.' It was the same advice he had given the think tank entrepreneur Antony Fisher.

With the Society's purpose settled, there followed a decade of more meetings: Beauvallon, France in 1951, Seelisberg again in 1953, Venice, Italy in 1954, Berlin, West Germany in 1956, St Moritz, Switzerland in 1957, Princeton, New Jersey in 1958 and Oxford, England in 1959. And the Society continued to grow in both membership and geographical spread; by 1961 there were 258 members, including several from Japan, South America, South Africa and New Zealand.

Capitalism and the Historians

A single exception was made to the no-publishing rule. Members were so impressed by papers delivered to the Society on the theme of history and capitalism that Hayek was asked to turn them into a book.

Capitalism and the Historians, published commercially in 1963, proved a great success. It showed how historians had chronically misrepresented the effects of England's Industrial Revolution on the population. Historians, it argued, were rewriting history to remake history – distorting the facts in the attempt to prove that capitalism had driven down the living standards of the working class. In fact, the book's authors observed, workers were flocking from the farms and into the industrial towns, which gave them wider employment opportunities, a more secure living in better conditions, better and regular pay, and greater access to facilities, community life and education than they ever could have had working on the land.

Unresolved and emerging issues

Despite the Society's successes, by the 1959 Oxford meeting more divisions were emerging. Hayek wanted to hand over as President, but the obvious successors, Jewkes and Röpke, did not wish to take on the task, so Hayek was persuaded to continue. Disagreements about the size of the Society also resurfaced: should it be small and elite or large and inclusive? Some members worried that the Society's size was now inhibiting discussion. 'Unlimited growth,' Hayek agreed, 'may change the character of the Society entirely.'

There was debate too when Hunold began publishing *The Mont Pelerin Quarterly* in 1959. There was no agreement over whether the *Quarterly* should be a learned journal, a policy broadsheet or a members' newsletter, and, as we shall see in the next chapter, this would not end well for Hunold. Questions began to be raised. What exactly were his responsibilities? Was he in reality the Society's Chief Executive? If so, how far did his authority extend? And how far should it extend? These would be the most bitter questions that the Society ever faced.

MPS Nobelist No. 5 (1988) Maurice Allais (1911–2010)

Allais was a prolific economist who made important contributions to the theories of general equilibrium, capital, decision-making, money and probability. His work anticipated that of better-known economists, such as Sir John Hicks and Paul Samuelson, but was underappreciated because he wrote in French rather than English, the preferred language of economics.

Originally a professor at France's École des Mines (and later head of the National Centre for Economic Research in the US), he is best known for his work on efficient pricing in large monopolistic enterprises, such as state-owned industries. He sought ways to balance social benefits with economic efficiency through the pricing strategies of state monopolies (e.g. mining and utilities) rather than regulation.

However, his focus was on economic efficiency, whether it was in markets or in the state-industry sector. He identified equilibrium in a market economy as the point of maximum efficiency and held that maximum efficiency is also an equilibrium point.

In relation to capital theory, he elucidated the trade-offs between present and future productivity and argued that real income grows most efficiently when interest rates equal growth rates. He explored the supply of money and the demand to hold it, arguing that this explains business cycles – work redolent of that of Hayek and Friedman. His work on risk-management behaviour led to the Allais Paradox, that lower risks were less attractive to speculators.

6 THE HUNOLD AFFAIR

Until 1959 the Society had been essentially a two-person operation. Hayek, as President, initiated and managed the intellectual content, while Hunold, as Secretary, raised money and managed the administration. But increasingly, Hunold was beginning to take charge.

In his native Switzerland, Hunold was a man of some status: an intellectual as well as a successful business executive. He felt entitled to high status in the Mont Pelerin Society too. He was not just a founding member; it was his funding initiative that breathed life into the Society in the first place. His ability to raise money was crucial to the success of the subsequent meetings. He worked long and hard on running the Society. And he spent a lot of his own money keeping it going.

Princeton and Oxford

Hayek, meanwhile, was keen to strengthen the Society's American links. He planned a US meeting in 1953 but could not raise the necessary funds. Yet by 1958, Machlup had secured finance for a meeting in Princeton, New Jersey, which, he claimed, would be the largest and most elaborate event yet held.

And so it was. But its impending success threatened to eclipse Hunold. Behind the scenes, he subjected the American organisers to constant interference and criticism. The principal donor, Jasper Crane of the DuPont Company, complained of Hunold's 'rudeness' and how he 'quarrelled with everyone in Princeton'.

Hunold also circulated a personal memoir, *The Story of the Mont Pelerin Society*, which – to the dismay of several prominent members – disparaged the prominent Austrian–American economist Joseph Schumpeter, who had earlier dismissed the Society as irrelevant. Machlup regarded Hunold's attack on Schumpeter as unworthy of a member of the Society. Hayek said that he too was 'thoroughly fed up' with Hunold's conduct – even though he accepted that Hunold was 'indispensable for the administration of the Society'.

Hunold certainly felt himself indispensable, particularly in the running of meetings. He had raised money for and organised previous meetings. He had arranged everything, including the programme, for the successful 1956 Berlin meeting. His experience and success in the administration of meetings convinced him that he should be the final authority on such things.

But the Oxford meeting in 1959 was even more acrimonious than the Princeton one. Hunold complained to Antony Fisher, one of its key UK sponsors, that the conference was too English, with too many British speakers and no translation services. He grumbled that it focused too much on economics. He wanted other speakers invited. He also objected that Ralph Harris, whom Fisher had hired to run the Institute of Economic Affairs, was centrally involved in planning the meeting, even though he was not (yet) a member.

Hunold came to believe there was an Anglo-American conspiracy to replace him with the popular and energetic Harris. He opposed Harris's membership and wrote to Board members, disparaging the role of Harris and the Institute of Economic Affairs in the Oxford conference. He demanded a re-vote when Harris's membership was agreed. A flurry of heated exchanges followed.

The *Quarterly*

One area where Hunold seemed answerable to no one, however, was his publishing of the *Quarterly*. This was not a cheap venture (its costs far exceeded the $877 income of the Society) and was only made possible through Hunold's fund-raising. He raised enough money to keep the *Quarterly* going from 1959 to 1962.

Hunold's third issue of the *Quarterly* in January 1960 inflamed the earlier tensions further. Hayek protested that, against Council policy, it expressed editorial opinions – and even attacked individual members of the Society. Hunold, however, insisted on retaining his editorial independence and control.

For Hayek, it was the last straw. He saw further collaboration with Hunold as impossible, and he told Röpke (who remained Hunold's staunch supporter) of his intention to resign as President. With it clear that either Hunold or Hayek would have to go, factions began to coalesce and votes were canvassed. A circular to the whole membership from Hunold, to which Hayek replied in another, made all members acutely aware of the dispute and of just how deep it was.

The Society's eleventh meeting, organised by Röpke and Hunold, took place in Kassel, West Germany in 1960. It was opened by Ludwig Erhard, the economics minister who had abolished the post-war wage and price controls and unleashed West Germany's 'economic miracle'. Hunold saw the meeting as an opportunity to proclaim the practical importance and success of liberal policies, and ensured that European and American newspaper reporters were present – to the discomfort of members who believed that the Society should not appear so public and political.

Intellectually, the meeting was a success, but the internal conflict raged. Erhard had to step in as peacemaker. It was not easy; Hunold felt he had every right to continue, but Hayek would accept no solution that left Hunold in power.

Compromises and departures

Eventually a compromise was reached in which both Hayek and Hunold stepped down from their offices, Röpke became interim President, the Italian political scientist and lawyer Bruno Leoni became European Secretary, and Hunold became Vice President and continued to produce the *Quarterly*. But as Hartwell observed: 'It is doubtful that

Hunold would have accepted the solution he did without the influence of Erhard's prestige and authority, to which even Hunold deferred.'

Even so, the conflict soon erupted again with Hunold's minutes of the Kassel agreement, which differed crucially from what others thought had been decided. The discord resurfaced again at the 1961 meeting in Turin, Italy. The Treasurer, the American social scientist Clarence E. Philbrook, was affronted by Hunold's suggestion that payments for the travel expenses of American participants at Kassel had been made illegally. Friedman, meanwhile, objected to the undignified remarks about John Kenneth Galbraith, the critic of American capitalism, that appeared in the *Quarterly*. There were arguments about the site of the next meeting, and how far Hunold should be involved. There was even friction over the order in which the Vice Presidents should be listed, and therefore, by implication, how high Hunold ranked.

By 1962, relations between Hunold and other Board members had irretrievably broken down. On seeing the January 1962 edition of the *Quarterly*, the Board disowned it. Hayek, Leoni and the Americans on the Council concluded that they could not 'any further remain in the same Society with Dr Hunold'. For his part, Hunold still had many supporters, including important ones such as the President, Röpke, and the American businessman and philanthropist Pierre Goodrich, who had continued to fund the *Quarterly*. But the situation was untenable. There were moves to exclude Hunold from the Society entirely, led by the British business economist Arthur Shenfield and by

Machlup, who was even prepared to see Röpke excluded for supposedly being untrue to the Kassel agreement.

Under pressure to stand down, Röpke resigned – not just from office but from the Society too – and Hunold followed him out soon after. Hunold's resignation, says Hartwell, 'ended both the conflict within the Society and the financial embarrassment the *Quarterly* could have become'.

MPS Nobelist No. 6 (1991) Ronald Coase (1910–2013)

Coase was a pioneer in the economic study of transaction costs, social costs and public goods. A common theme was that economists' abstract mathematical models largely ignored institutions that were crucial to how the world really worked. His focus on such institutions led to him becoming editor of the *Journal of Law and Economics.*

His fame centres around three seminal articles. In 'The Nature of the Firm' (1937), Coase (then a socialist) asked why, when economists saw markets in terms of freewheeling transactions between individuals, the dominant reality was firms – groups cooperating under management. He answered that economists were wrong in assuming that transactions are costless: transaction costs could be large, and firms existed to economise on them. Transaction cost analysis became a completely new field.

In 'The Problem of Social Cost' (1960), Coase critiqued the presumption that disputes about externalities could always be resolved efficiently. He argued that transaction costs meant that the outcomes depended crucially on how property rights were assigned. Hence the need for institutions (like courts) that were largely ignored by economists.

In 'The Lighthouse in Economics' (1974), Coase criticised the standard theory that public goods (e.g. lighthouses), where access was impossible to control, would not be produced except by government. He pointed out real cases where lighthouses were privately owned and operated, thanks to institutional arrangements that allowed ships to be billed in harbour.

7   THE MEETINGS OF THE 1950s

Intellectual concerns again

The Hunold conflicts cast a pall over meetings that were otherwise considerable intellectual successes. The Turin meeting, for example, grappled with the public criticism of large-scale enterprises, especially multinationals, which had come to be seen as the main cause of the continuing dependency and poverty of the less developed economies. The participants felt that economic change and the rise in services would bring more opportunities for small firms. Mises, characteristically, rejected all state subsidies to businesses of any size, calling support for small businesses and farms a 'romantic middle-class policy'. But the German liberals were keener to preserve a balance in the treatment of large and small firms.

Another issue discussed in Turin was the worrying efforts of the Soviet Union to ingratiate itself with the governments and citizens of less developed countries. How should liberal countries respond? Not by pumping in aid of their own, argued Brandt; rather, the West should aim to give these countries a vision of freedom and the benefits of markets over wasteful state spending, and to open up to these countries through more active trade and less protectionism.

As often before, the debate on the international monetary system produced most disagreement. Some wanted a return to the gold standard; Friedman and Machlup favoured flexible exchange rates. The only consensus was the need for stability. Monetary policy has been a continuing debate among members of the Society.

A second conflict

On a personal level, a new conflict was brewing between Jewkes and Leoni, the new President and Secretary. A disagreement about the site of the next conference developed into yet another dispute about the relative power of office-bearers. After the 1962 Knokke meeting in Belgium, Jewkes thought it important to have another meeting in 1963. 'Leoni wanted to have a conference imaginatively sited on a boat sailing on the Rhine … or in France,' reports Hartwell, 'but could not be certain of obtaining the necessary funds.' So Jewkes proposed instead another meeting in Oxford.

The Board and Council supported Oxford, but Leoni objected, saying that the facilities and food in France were far superior (points on which he was almost certainly correct). And perhaps he thought that returning to England might reinforce the perceived Anglo-American domination of the Society.

Jewkes eventually defused the tension with a long conciliatory letter to Leoni, but this relative calm came too late to save the 1963 Oxford conference proposal. Fearing that pressing on with Oxford would simply perpetuate the disagreement, Jewkes had cancelled it, bitterly blaming the loss on Leoni's 'persistent and determined opposition'. However, the Austrian philanthropist Max Thurn filled the gap by offering to organise a 1964 meeting in Semmering, Austria.

Moving on and outward

The Semmering conference was a great success. Attended by 240 members and guests, it epitomised the growth in the Society and the spread of members' ideas. Past disputes were put aside, and a new and more businesslike constitution was adopted, allowing the Society to concentrate on its intellectual task.

But as the meetings grew in size, so did the problems of financing them. Funds were usually raised from local sources, since the Society had limited resources of its own from which to fund conferences or meet deficits. A proposed 1965 meeting in Venezuela had to be abandoned because of a lack of finance, though Leoni was able to organise a meeting in Stresa, Italy for that year.

The new Board elected in Stresa was more international than before, including as it did both a Central American and a Japanese member alongside the Europeans and Americans. Also at Stresa, plans were agreed for an ambitious new venture: a Special Meeting in Tokyo, Japan, as proposed by Hayek's student Chiaki Nishiyama.

Funding the travel of American and European programme participants in Tokyo would be a big challenge for the organisers of the Japan meeting; but a grant from the

Reim Foundation helped, and the event was another great success. Japan now became an important national focus for the Society. There would be other meetings in Japan in 1988 and 2008.

Setbacks and successes

Meanwhile, plans were agreed for a meeting in Vichy, France and another in Aviemore, Scotland. Meetings were now coming thick and fast.

Yet there were setbacks. In late 1967, the new President, Bruno Leoni, was murdered by a person who his law firm was pursuing for unpaid rent. Ralph Harris, now planning the 1968 Aviemore meeting, informed the Board of this tragic setback and suggested that the Senior Vice President, French economist Daniel Villey, should take over. But Villey had a heart condition and was reluctant. So too was Friedman, who had too many other commitments. Eventually the German economist Friedrich Lutz, a past President, was persuaded to fill the gap on an interim basis.

Nevertheless, these setbacks did not prevent a successful meeting in Aviemore going ahead; and the Society branched out again with a 1969 Latin American meeting in Caracas, Venezuela. It seemed that the Society could look forward with confidence to celebrating its twenty-fifth anniversary.

MPS Nobelist No. 7 (1992) Gary S. Becker (1930–2014)

Becker systematically applied rational choice theory and micro-economic analysis to a wide range of human behaviour normally studied by sociologists, including the family, crime, addiction, migration, organ donation, discrimination and education.

He pioneered human capital theory, arguing in his book *Human Capital* (1964) that education and training were investments in 'human' capital, raising the individual's potential productivity just as physical capital does for firms.

He also explored business decisions, such as when firms discriminate against particular groups of job candidates. This, he observed, raised their costs by limiting their choice – explaining why there is less discrimination in highly competitive markets than in uncompetitive ones.

Becker used microeconomics to describe the competition between interest groups in terms of the benefits to tax recipients (e.g. subsidised businesses) versus the costs to taxpayers and the economy more generally. He argued that these costs outpaced the benefits, setting an upper limit to the size of government.

He argued that criminals' decisions whether to commit crimes depended on the perceived costs and benefits at the time. Anti-crime strategies should focus on efficiently altering that choice, for example, by increasing the likelihood of detection, the speed of prosecution and the severity of punishment. And he applied microeconomic analysis to personal decisions, such as whether to be an organ donor and when people choose to marry or have children.

8 THE CHALLENGES OF THE 1970s

Friedman's concerns

Could the Society really be confident about celebrating its twenty-fifth anniversary? Some members were still uneasy about its growth – including Friedman, one of the founder members, who in 1970 would become its first non-European President. He thought the upcoming twenty-fifth anniversary in 1972 was a good opportunity to take stock, and he circulated his views and concerns to members.

Friedman pointed out that the number of people now attending meetings meant that venues were overloaded, such that participants found themselves spread between different hotels, which inhibited 'free-wheeling discussion'. Large meetings also required years of planning: could the Society count on volunteers coming forward each time? And, he went on, the large-scale format had deadened the debate: meetings had become 'tourist attractions' rather than lively and exciting intellectual debates.

To discuss these issues, Friedman arranged a Special Board Meeting in Montreux in 1971, with about a dozen other senior members in attendance. Friedman himself was sceptical about the Society's future. On the plus side, he argued, it served four important functions: it put liberals in communication with each other; it stimulated the exchange of ideas; it promoted learning; and it helped create a greater understanding of the foundations of a free society. Yet he also felt that if it could not recreate the spirit, intimacy and intellectual thrill of the early meetings, the Society might be better to go out 'in a blaze of glory'.

The Board was not minded to disband the Society; after all, the threat to freedom was still profound, and liberal principles still needed to be refined and spread. Instead, the Board resolved to limit recruitment, screen applicants more thoroughly and control the size and format of meetings. It also agreed to raise an endowment to maintain a permanent secretariat to help relieve the pressures on officers and meeting organisers.

In the event, not all these resolutions were carried out. The Society and its meetings continued to grow in size and the pursuit of an endowment was at best half-hearted.

The anniversary meeting

The 1972 anniversary meeting, also in Montreux, included a pilgrimage to nearby Mont-Pèlerin, where (wrote Friedman later) Hayek was 'moved profoundly and in turn moved the rest of us by his remarks'. The programme, drawn up by Friedman's Chicago colleague George J. Stigler (another founder member), debated the principal problems facing liberal economists at the time – inflation, trade unions, growth, trade and the media. A significant presentation at this event came from the American public choice economist James M. Buchanan, who explained his thoughts on the economics of political and bureaucratic decision-making – ideas that, fourteen years later, would win him the Nobel Prize in Economic Science.

The Montreux meeting was also a chance for the membership to confirm the structural decisions taken at the Special Board Meeting in 1971. It was decided that a new committee would review future membership applications. Registration fees would rise substantially; and members would no longer be fully subsidised. Local committees would become largely responsible for the finance and organisation of meetings.

A paid assistant secretary

The Board also moved to deal with the strain of central administration – a problem about which Hunold had complained years before. It appointed the Luxembourg business economist Jean-Pierre Hamilius as a salaried assistant secretary, with the dual role of organising European meetings and producing a newsletter to keep members up to date with the Society's activities, and each other's.

But this first venture into having a paid secretariat turned out unhappily. Board members tended to load work onto Hamilius as their paid executive, so most of the organisation of the 1973 Regional Meeting in Salzburg, Austria – including translating papers between French and German – fell to him. At the same time, Hamilius felt a duty to produce a frequent and high-quality newsletter. The burden of all these competing obligations began to overwhelm him.

Hamilius was exhausted, but he carried on. After all, there was the 1974 General Meeting set for Brussels to organise – though this time the local Belgian members did more of the work. But there was one more difficult task for Hamilius to do: namely, to secure from Hunold the early records of the Society. Fortunately he succeeded in this delicate task. These records, including the extensive album of photographs that Hunold took at the original 1947 meeting, are now archived in the Hoover Institution in Palo Alto, California. Today the Hoover Institution archive also contains most of the subsequent correspondence, minutes, programmes and other documents of the Society.

By the mid 1970s, the cost of Hamilius's ambitious *Newsletter*, along with his other expenses, were rising. The Society was living well beyond its means. By 1977 the Treasurer, American economics professor Arthur Kemp, was sufficiently alarmed to propose abandoning both the post of Assistant Secretary and the *Newsletter*. By way of compromise, George Stigler, as President, wrote to Hamilius, capping his expenditure and suggesting that the *Newsletter* should appear just once a year.

But Hamilius, proud of what he had created, resigned indignantly. The office of Assistant Secretary lapsed and the *Newsletter* disappeared for a time before being revived in a less ambitious format. But at least the Society was again spared another potential financial embarrassment.

Financial management

Even so, managing the Society's financial affairs was no easy task. Today, the accounts are professionally audited and filed. But every year during the 1960s and 1970s, Philbrook and Kemp, during their respective terms as Treasurer, both had doubts about whether the Society's financial records would meet the stringent requirements of the US tax authorities. In fact, though, the accounts passed official scrutiny and the Society's tax-exempt status was never challenged.

Philbrook and Kemp's main problem was to get the Europeans to take the American accounting standards and legal requirements seriously. Following the departure of Hunold, who raised most of the early funds, Leoni became the main fundraiser for the European meetings; but after Leoni's untimely death in 1967, his successor Ralph Harris described Leoni's papers as voluminous but 'rather patchy'.

Not that Harris was a meticulous record keeper himself. Kemp found him 'genial but elusive' – complaining of him doing just enough, just in time, to allow Kemp to file the annual tax return. But even that small measure of compliance required constant hounding from Kemp, who expressed his frustration on several occasions. Harris, meanwhile, resented the Society's finances being run entirely from the US; to him it reinforced the feeling of American dominance, and (in those days before email or even fax machines) it made the Society's financial operations difficult, slow and clumsy. Harris and Villey had even suggested creating a European Treasurer – an idea firmly slapped down by Philbrook.

The cost of meetings

Another issue was to clarify the Society's financial responsibility for meetings. Before Kemp, the accounts for meetings were intermingled with those of the Society, which left the financial records confused and raised issues for the Society's US tax status. Kemp insisted on separate accounts for all meetings – a rule which persists to this day. But even then, he (like his predecessors) was rarely consulted on the financial plans for meetings, merely presented with the accounts and the bills.

That changed only when Edwin J. Feulner Jr, the experienced head of the Heritage Foundation in Washington, took over as Treasurer in 1979. Today, the Society's Treasurer plays a key role in the financial planning of meetings and in raising financial support for them, particularly support to help young scholars to attend.

Finance for meetings has always posed problems. The early meetings were free to participants – something that was important to many, particularly the Germans, because of the currency controls then in force. But at Seelisberg in 1953, for the first time, members had to pay for their own accommodation; and thereafter, that became the usual practice. The rising costs of conference venues large enough for the group meant that, from the 1972 Montreux meeting onwards, participants have also been charged a registration fee. Even with most participants paying their own way, however, substantial funds still have to be raised towards the organisation and conduct of the meetings, which in many cases are five or more days long.

MPS Nobelist No. 8 (2002) Vernon L. Smith (1927–)

Over his long academic career, Smith became a leading contributor to behavioural economics and a pioneer of experimental economics, for which he earned the Nobel Prize in Economic Science.

Raised on a farm in Kansas, he went on to earn degrees from several universities, including a PhD from Harvard. He went on to hold a number of academic appointments and was on the editorial boards of several economic journals, including the *American Economic Review* and the *Journal of Economic Behavior and Organization*.

Smith advanced the use of laboratory experiments, in which subjects were given practical economic choices, to gain a better understanding of how real-world economic choices are made, and how different conditions may affect them. By changing the parameters under which lab-based 'market' choices are made, for example, we may be able to identify which rules and institutions make real-world markets operate more (or less) efficiently.

Such techniques demonstrate that our economic institutions are critical to the way in which markets work. They also allow us to assess the value of different institutions empirically, with a view to selecting the most efficient or desirable. For example, economists can assess how different trading arrangements, such as different kinds of auction, affect the allocation of scarce resources.

9   GROWTH AND RECOGNITION

Bleak as the prospects for liberalism still appeared to be at the twenty-fifth anniversary meeting in 1972, liberal ideas were about to come into the ascendancy, bringing the Society further growth and greater recognition. The 1970s brought Nobel prizes for Hayek and Friedman – followed by more in the 1980s for Stigler, Buchanan and Allais.

New people and new places

By the late 1970s a new generation was running the Society. Feulner's election as Treasurer was crucial; a proven fundraiser and capable administrator, he took over at a time when funding for meetings was becoming vital, and accounting standards were growing more onerous. He became directly involved in the financial planning of conferences, and more of the general administration of the Society came to rest on his shoulders. He would bear the main burden of the Society's administration for over 30 years.

A pattern emerged, still followed now, of General Meetings (the main international meetings of the Society) being held in even-numbered years and one or more Regional Meetings (designed mainly for participants from particular hemispheres or continents) in odd-numbered years. Thus, in the 1970s there were five General Meetings and seven Regional Meetings, and the same again in the 1980s.

Among those events was the 1978 General Meeting in Hong Kong, the first General Meeting to be held outside Europe and the US. Feulner raised significant funds, and over a hundred members, together with twice that number of guests, attended the meeting. Moreover, the meeting elected as its new President Manuel Ayau, head of the Universidad Francisco Marroquín in Guatemala, which was (wrote Hartwell) 'a significant move indicating the changing character of the Society, particularly since he was succeeded by Nishiyama, a Japanese'.

Continuing debates

Some things did not change – for example, the continuing worries and debates about the Society's finances. In 1979 the American law and economics professor Henry Manne called for a significant increase in fees for non-academics, along with honoraria for the academic presenters. The academic members, he argued, were giving up their time to deliver 'one of the world's finest programmes', which the non-academics enjoyed at 'a ludicrous price'. The idea was firmly rejected by Ayau. Members, he said, did not agree to speak for a fee, but to 'enlighten and to assist those scholars, businessmen, journalists, etc., who are doing something important throughout the world, in their respective spheres of influence'.

A new disagreement arose over the suggestion of a meeting in Taipei, Taiwan. Feulner visited Taiwan and found 'a positive response' to the idea both there and in Washington. But it caused problems for Japanese members, and there were concerns that the Society might stumble into a political minefield, given the hostility between China and Taiwan. Friedman, true to form, argued that the Society should take no account of such politics and go ahead. In the event, Nishiyama defused the concerns by suggesting a meeting in Tokyo for 1977, which the Taiwanese could attend. Eventually, at the 1976 General Meeting in St Andrews, Scotland (held there to mark the 200th anniversary of Adam Smith's *The Wealth of Nations*), it was decided that Nishiyama would organise the General Meeting in Hong Kong in 1978, and that it would be preceded by what was termed a Special Meeting in Taipei.

Both meetings went ahead as planned. A decade later, in 1988, another meeting was held in Taipei. Again, it was not a formal Regional Meeting but another Special Meeting of Society members who were also attending the 1988 Tokyo/Kyoto General Meeting in Japan.

Growth without (much) disagreement

The 1980s was a decade of growth without great disagreement. Membership rose, meetings were held regularly, and attendance was high. The finances improved, thanks largely to Feulner's fundraising skills and prudent management. He brought in a number of generous donations, which not only helped towards the Society's meetings and organisational costs, but also provided for a new Hayek Essay Prize and for travel funds to promote the attendance of young scholars.

As Friedman had observed years before, because of the size and international nature of the Society, meetings needed to be held in large and convenient venues, which generally meant specialist conference hotels in capital city centres. And those were usually expensive. Now, with the cost of meetings continuing to rise, and amid concerns to safeguard the Society's funds, the Board decided that it would not consider offers to host a meeting unless there were firm assurances of financial support. In addition, meeting organisers would be subject to a much higher level of financial scrutiny by the Treasurer than in previous decades.

The Board also decided that membership dues should always be high enough to cover the costs of the *Newsletter*, which had re-emerged under a series of editors. In those pre-email times, printing and mailing copies of the *Newsletter* to several hundred members, located all around the world, was a significantly expensive venture. The printed Membership Directory, listing members' contact details, which again had to be mailed to all members, was another considerable expense.

The discussions about the Society's finances, running and organisation continued. A committee under Manne, like others before it, failed to come up with acceptable suggestions. But with things going well there was little agitation for change. For example, Friedman – still concerned about how the Society was expanding – suggested creating a 'Senate' of 'older and wiser heads' to act in an advisory role; but even this modest idea was not taken up until the 2012 General Meeting in Prague, before being abandoned again just four years later.

Size and publicity

With a clutch of Nobel prizes going to members in the 1970s and 1980s, the Society's international status rose considerably. Its fame spread and its meetings grew still more. Predictably, this brought problems beyond the perennial debate about the size and intimacy of the discussions. A number of other groups, some in which Society members were involved, were now fixing their own meetings around those of the Society, using that synergy to attract the Society's participants and speakers to their own events. The Board moved to discourage this, worried that the Society's reputation might be sullied, particularly if it came to be associated with the views of these other, sometimes political, organisations.

Since the 2002 London meeting, however, the Board has accepted that there can indeed be considerable benefits from coinciding with other meetings, at least with those organised by liberal but non-political bodies, such as friendly think tanks, foundations and groups of young scholars who might be potential future members. Though the policy is kept under review, such 'fringe' events are now generally welcomed rather than being discouraged.

Media interest was another issue raised by the growing recognition of the Society and of its individual members.

Many of those members were now internationally known – even famous. Fearing that media interest and reporting of meetings would inhibit the participants from speaking frankly, the Board moved quickly to curb such activities, emphasising the essentially private nature of the discussions.

The Chatham House Rule – a ban attributing remarks to any individual speaker – continues to apply at the Society's meetings, even in this age of instant communication. The only exceptions are some set-piece speeches and presentations, which are recorded and shared, or even broadcast live, online. But these exceptions are made only with the agreement of the Board and the members present.

Discussion about presentations, however, is still generally subject to the non-reporting rule. The idea is that members can safely put forward ideas that may not yet be fully formed and that they can discuss controversial issues without fear of being quoted or having their remarks taken out of context. Meetings are not *secret*, but in the interests of free speech and candour, the discussion remains *private*. Accordingly, while prominent members are often in demand for interviews, these always take place outside of the conference hall and never reveal what any individual might have said within it.

MPS Nobelist No. 9 (2010) Mario Vargas Llosa (1936–)

Peruvian-born Vargas Llosa is a prolific writer of novels, plays and essays that often explore themes of individual resistance and revolt and show his commitment to social change.

Originally a Marxist supporter of Castro's Cuban revolution, his later book *My Intellectual Journey* (2014) describes his subsequent move to liberalism, having realised that socialism was incompatible with liberty and freedom. In this, he was influenced by fellow Peruvian (and Society member) Hernando de Soto, whom he helped to establish the Institute for Liberty and Democracy in Lima.

His career began with a three-act play and stories in literary magazines. His prize-winning first novel *The City and the Dogs* describes a group of military academy cadets trying to navigate a corrupt, hostile regime – a metaphor for Peruvian politics itself. A later novel, *Conversation in the Cathedral*, describing a search for truth about a murder, attacked the dictatorial government of Manuel Odría. Another, *War of the End of the World,* was set against the backdrop of nineteenth-century conflicts in Brazil. Later, he moved on to write satires, parodies and humorous works, plus critical studies of writers including Flaubert, Camus and Sartre.

In 1990 he stood as President of Peru, losing to Alberto Fujimori. Three years later he became a Spanish citizen, living in Madrid, but still frequently visits and writes about Peru.

10 FREEDOM AND EXPANSION

Into Eastern Europe

In the 1980s and 1990s, members of the Society remained well aware that freedom was still under threat in large parts of the world; yet they had the exhilarating feeling that things were at last going their way. Several countries, starting with Margaret Thatcher's government in Britain, were privatising their state industries on a grand scale; governments from China to India and the US to France were cutting taxes, liberalising or retrenching; and progress was being made on tariff reductions and the liberalisation of international trade.

Then in 1989, with astonishing speed, came the most remarkable phenomenon of all. In May that year, Hungary's border guards began dismantling the barbed wire fortifications of the Iron Curtain, in advance of the Hungarian government's lifting of travel restrictions to Austria. By September, tens of thousands of East Germans were travelling through Hungary, then making their way into the free West. With the remainder of the Iron Curtain fortifications now rendered pointless, thousands of protestors began to congregate at the most symbolic part of the East–West divide: the Berlin Wall that had separated the city since

1961, which members had seen for themselves at the 1982 General Meeting in Berlin. Faced with the inevitable reality of the situation, in November 1989 the East German government announced that its citizens were now free to cross the border into West Germany. With hammers, pickaxes and any other tools they could find, the crowds tore down the Wall. They faced no resistance. Eastern Europe could be free again.

The 1990 General Meeting took place in Munich, which was still officially located in West Germany, but would soon be part of a reunited Germany. The theme was Europe in an Open World Order and the mood was upbeat. Speakers from Eastern Europe were invited, among them Václav Klaus, who would subsequently become Prime Minister and then President of the Czech Republic. But at Munich he attended as a mere economist, as unsure of the Society as it was of him.

With Eastern Europe now opening up, plans were laid for a 1991 Regional Meeting in Prague, Czechoslovakia. It was premature to imagine that freedom was now completely safe, but there was a feeling that the Society's hard and long effort was at last paying off. Other meetings would take place in the former Soviet bloc countries: in Potsdam, (East) Germany in 1999, Bratislava, Slovakia in 2001, and Prague again in 2012.

The death of Hayek

Yet the euphoria of the times was tinged by sadness at the passing in 1992 of the Society's founder, Friedrich Hayek.

He had lived just long enough to see the Iron Curtain fall and Soviet collectivism – its dismal workings and results now thrust into full and undeniable view – thoroughly discredited. His death was marked by a brief ceremony at the 1992 General Meeting in Vancouver, Canada. The 1994 General Meeting in Cannes, France became an opportunity to review a number of Hayek's most productive themes – spontaneous order, business cycles, capitalism and the historians, and the ethics of freedom.

The 1996 General Meeting in Vienna, Austria, however, looked forward, discussing the liberal response to some very modern social policy issues: environment, healthcare, privatisation, corruption, crime and immigration. It seemed to be fully in line with Hayek's original hope of making liberal philosophy relevant to contemporary concerns.

And then it was time to mark another milestone – the fiftieth anniversary of the original meeting at Mont-Pèlerin, observed in a small members-only meeting in the mountain resort itself, and celebrated with a much larger General Meeting in Washington, DC, in 1998.

Special meetings

The Society now launched itself into another new venture – a series of Special Meetings, initiated mainly by Greg Lindsay of the Centre for Independent Studies in Australia and Linda Whetstone, a Board member of the Atlas Economic Research Foundation and daughter of the Foundation's founder, Antony Fisher. (In 1988, shortly before his death,

Fisher was knighted at the recommendation of Margaret Thatcher, becoming Sir Antony Fisher.)

The aim of these Special Meetings was to open up new countries to liberal ideas and to scout for potential new members in places where the Society was under-represented, such as Bali, Indonesia (1999), Goa, India (2002), Colombo and Kandalama, Sri Lanka (2004), Nairobi, Kenya (2007), New Delhi, India (2011) and Fez, Morocco (2012). Alongside the 2011 Regional Meeting in Istanbul, Turkey, the Fez conference marked an attempt to explore the relevance of liberal ideas in Islamic countries. A 2012 meeting on evolution and economics, imaginatively sited in the Galapagos Islands, also broke new intellectual ground, focusing on the potential cross-fertilisation be-tween the natural and social sciences.

Experienced fundraisers and organisers from policy think tanks, such as Feulner and Lindsay, were by now playing a larger part in the Society's affairs. As meetings grew larger and costlier, it became more difficult for indi-vidual academics to organise and finance them. Since the Vienna, Austria meeting in 1996, all General Meetings have been run by hosts with the backup of a research institute or similar body.

These changes are also reflected in the Society's officers. Apart from Hunold, almost all of the early Board and Council members were academics. Now it is common to see think tank executives and intellectuals from business, journalism and the law on the Board.

They feature as senior officers too. The first non-academic to be elected President of the Society was

Harris – by then ennobled (also at the recommendation of Margaret Thatcher) to Lord Harris of High Cross in 1979. More recently there have been several other non-academic presidents: Feulner in 1996, the Uruguayan lawyer Ramón Diaz in 1998, Greg Lindsay in 2006 and Linda Whetstone in 2020.

Other innovations

Meetings changed and developed too, with new ideas being trialled and then developed. The 2002 General Meeting in London, England featured lunch 'topic tables' and after-hours meetings to allow for more intimate and detailed discussion on subjects chosen by members. Great effort was put into providing scholarships for young people. Roving microphones replaced the traditional standing microphones to help maintain the flow of the debate. The London conference was held over a weekend instead of during the week to help members with work commitments. The traditional excursion – a staple ever since the first meeting in Mont-Pèlerin – was moved from the middle to the end of the meeting so as to condense the formal part of the event for the benefit of busy members. And, in those days before wi-fi, an Internet café provided online computer access for those who wanted to keep in touch with their offices back home.

Other meeting organisers experimented too. For example, though the Society's members had become used to meeting in prominent international hotels in capital city centres, the organisers of the 2009 Regional Meeting in

Stockholm took the step of booking a smaller and cheaper hotel so that extra funds could be devoted to scholarships. The resulting large presence of young scholars was reckoned a considerable success and provided a model for future events.

Some of these changes were repeated in subsequent meetings, others not. For example, the Internet café provision, itself a technological innovation, was made redundant by further rapid advances in online connectivity. The topic tables have reappeared and disappeared at various times. Young scholars' programmes have become a standard and vital part of meetings. But conferences have mostly reverted to during the working week, and the idea of moving the excursion did not catch on; ever since the first meeting, which featured one half-day and two full-day excursions, the informal outings have been regarded as a key opportunity to promote greater personal connection between members – particularly between those of different generations – and is seen an integral part of the meetings' purpose, rather than a mere bolt-on extra.

Reaffirmation and improvement

The activities and aims of the Society were reviewed again at an informal meeting of the Board and senior members held at the 2005 Regional Meeting in Reykjavik, Iceland. They proposed that the membership committee should act as 'talent scouts', and that there was a need to attract people from additional countries, with perhaps more

Special Meetings like those already held in Bali, Goa and Sri Lanka.

The Board also resolved that membership nominations should be made online – a new Society website was now up and running – and that there should be a fast-track membership process for prominent liberal thinkers, even if they had not attended earlier meetings (as the existing rules demanded). Membership applications would be reviewed twice a year, instead of only every two years at General Meetings. But in the event, it took more than a decade for the Society to make its membership application process paperless; fast-track membership was adopted, but later abandoned amid concerns that it created members who were not really very interested in the Society's activities; and membership applications eventually moved to a more manageable and less exhausting annual round.

There was debate too in Reykjavik on how to retain young members who came as Hayek Essay Prize scholars, but often then dropped out because of the high cost of attending international meetings. This remains a continuing problem, though much effort now goes into raising funds for scholarships available to young scholars, and retention rates have improved.

In another discussion redolent of Hayek's original proposals for a liberal 'academy', the group in Reykjavik agreed that the Society's intellectual programmes needed to be strengthened. Although its intellectual depth and breadth was seen as giving it a unique edge over other liberal-minded organisations that had grown up (often running their own international meetings), work was needed to maintain the Society's relevance. The group therefore called for meetings to address the current threats to liberty, such as regulation and populism, and explore the ethical and political case for freedom, not just the economic case.

Accordingly, there was a strong view that the Society should adhere to its intellectual purpose – though it should remain open to non-academics. As often before, the group in Reykjavik felt that the Society needed more non-economists in its membership, such as historians and philosophers. As Feulner had written in his 1999 *Intellectual Pilgrims*, 'This imbalance in our membership has never been rectified and may account for the fact that, while we have brilliantly succeeded in developing a critique of, and alternative to, economic interventionism, Hayek's goal of formulating a "comprehensive philosophy of freedom" continues to challenge us.'

11 TAKING ON THE CRITICS

New York

One of the biggest intellectual challenges for the Society in the first decade of the new millennium was an economic one: the financial crash of 2008. This was widely reported in the media and by intellectuals as a 'failure of capitalism'. Public faith in free markets took a severe blow, and there were numerous calls for Keynesian-style policies, involving more public spending, cheap credit and money creation.

There was a multitude of false narratives around the financial crisis. Some put it down to lax and insufficient regulation. Others even hailed it as the glorious self-destructive 'end of capitalism' predicted by Marx (albeit a century and a half earlier, and in a very different economic environment). The ease with which these narratives made their way into public and political consciousness convinced Mont Pelerin Society members (and other liberals too) of the importance of updating, developing and disseminating their ideas even more strongly and urgently.

For its part, the Society responded with a 2009 Special Meeting on the crisis, held in the world's leading financial centre, New York. Most participants there saw the crash as a crisis of politics, not markets. It was, they believed, the sad but inevitable result of a long and unsustainable boom created by the loose money and cheap credit policies of politicians and central bankers. Hayek, of course, had won his Nobel Prize largely for his 1930s work on just such boom–bust cycles.

The New York meeting marked the start of a concerted (but perhaps ultimately insufficient) intellectual fightback by free-marketeers to the criticism they suffered following the crash. The Austrian and monetarist views that boom–bust cycles were set off by an excess of credit or money were repeated and debated. *Forbes* publisher Steve Forbes scornfully debunked the notion that the crisis was caused by the 'greed' of bankers: we had been told for decades that bankers were greedy, so what had changed, he asked. And the Nobel economist Gary S. Becker proposed solutions to the 'too big to fail' problem, with more onerous reserve requirements on large banks, reflecting the systemic risk they pose, and lighter rules on smaller banks. This, he argued, would encourage greater competition – something that might have restrained the worst excesses of the boom years.

The returning threat

By 2012, keen to take on new allies (particularly younger and energetic ones) to help in the fightback, the Society had grown to around 600 members. Of those, a fifth had been added following a controversial Board decision, taken at the 2010 General Meeting in Sydney, Australia, to allow the Society's expansion up to 1,000 members. Development progressed on other fronts too. Through prudent management, and despite the financial crash, the Society's reserves were strong. And at last, Milton Friedman's idea of an advisory Senate was made a reality, with all past Presidents, Secretaries and Treasurers being designated as members of the body.

The 2012 General Meeting in Prague was a glittering affair, with meetings in Prague Castle, hosted by the President of the Czech Republic, Václav Klaus – the once-unknown East European economist who was the centre of so much bemused interest at the 1990 Munich meeting. But the 2012 event in Prague was more downbeat than the 1991 meeting held in the same city soon after the fall of the Iron Curtain. More than two decades on, members had become acutely aware of 'liberalism's manifest inability to translate its intellectual victories into political victories that seriously roll back the size and power of the socialist welfare state', as Feulner had put it.

'Ideas,' he had told the special 50th anniversary gathering in Mont-Pèlerin, 'are decisive, but not self-implementing.' Big government had been discredited intellectually, but government was still bigger than ever. Central planning had been abandoned, but a mass of suffocating regulations had filled the interventionist void. Soviet socialism might have ended, but there were new threats to freedom.

To the European members at the 2012 General Meeting, one of the greatest of these threats was, paradoxically, Western Europe itself – by then consolidated into a supranational body, the European Union. The Prague meeting focused on the growing centralisation and politicisation of the EU, its fondness for regulation, and the single European currency that was already raising tensions between different European countries and was making the post-crash economic adjustment that much more difficult. (For once, this was a discussion about currency that did not cause dissent.)

The Society's critics

The rising prominence of the Society and several of its members, coupled with its determination to keep its discussions private, has excited both legitimate critics of liberal ideas and the usual crop of conspiracy theorists. The latter imagine the Society as masterminding the activities of think tanks and politicians around the globe. Yet in reality, being only a discussion forum, it does not and cannot direct anyone. In any case, its members have generally nursed a long and healthy suspicion of politicians and political activists. The Italian communist Luciana Gallino and the US historian Philip Mirowski likewise suggest that the Society created a liberal intellectual hegemony in the world's universities. In fact, academics, particularly those in the social sciences, have always veered to the left; and with only two or three members in most countries, the Society hardly has a strong enough representation to dictate the policies of universities.

Critics also imagine the Society as a collection of rabid ultra-individualists – conveniently dismissed as 'neoliberals' – even though its members reflect a wide mixture of views. Since 1947, as mentioned, members have debated how far liberal thinking should be a 'pure' approach and how far it must be tempered by the current needs and values of society.

Other attempts to tarnish the Society's name delve 50 years into the past to associate it with the disgraced US President Richard Nixon and the Chilean dictator Augusto Pinochet, pointing out that Milton Friedman advised both. In a sense the association is true, though Friedman was happy to give *anyone* the benefit of his advice; and he dropped Nixon immediately when it was not followed. He had no formal or lasting relationship with Pinochet, and indeed criticised him on many fronts, both social and economic – though Hispanic students of his helped turn Chile, whatever its other faults, into the economically most prosperous country in South America.

Another line of attack, promoted by the British journalist George Monbiot and others, is that the Society is a conspiracy of the rich: that Hayek knew the ultra-rich would pay him to spread policy ideas that favoured them; and that the Society cultivated Ronald Reagan and Margaret Thatcher to get that agenda in place. The reality is very different. Hayek struggled to raise funds in 1947, and funding has been a problem for the Society ever since. In any case, the Society comprises mostly academics, not the wealthy elite, and their focus is more on liberating the working poor and on growing economies, not helping the already rich. As for Reagan and Thatcher (going back half a century again), the Society had no influence on them except through ideas, and if it expected them to slash public spending, cut the tax burden and restore a free-market paradise, it would have been left sadly disappointed. But Mont Pelerin Society members have never expected much except disappointment from politicians.

Personnel changes

In practical terms, the time around the 2012 General Meeting in Prague also marked the beginning of major changes in the Society's personnel and organisation.

Ill health forced Giancarlo Ibarguen of the Universidad Francisco Marroquín in Guatemala to step down from his role as Secretary of the Society in 2012. Eamonn Butler of the Adam Smith Institute agreed to take over.

Feulner too, after retiring from his post as President of the Heritage Foundation in 2013, also stepped down as its long-serving Treasurer and main organiser, though he continued to help greatly with fundraising. He nominated a worthy successor in Professor J. R. Clarke of the University of Tennessee. Running an international Society of around 600 members had become a very demanding and time-consuming job, most of it falling on the Treasurer. Clarke, however, had huge experience in managing large professional associations, being Treasurer of the Southern Economic Association and the Association of Private Enterprise Education (many of whose members were also members of the Mont Pelerin Society).

These changes came at a time of mounting concern about the sheer scale of the job of managing a growing, diverse, international body. Its officers, after all, were all volunteers. There was a rising view that the Board needed to become more open to new people, new ideas and new meeting formats – and to keep in better touch with the membership. In response to these challenges, Clarke sharpened the management and accounting, while Butler set about producing annual surveys of members' opinions on the Society's events, management and purpose.

12 SHAPING UP FOR
THE TWENTY-FIRST CENTURY

New thinking in Hong Kong

The Hong Kong General Meeting of 2014 brought the Society's members, who had previously rejoiced in China's liberalisation and accession to the world trading system, up against the realities of that revival. The local organiser, Yue-Chim Richard Wong, invited the former Chief Executive of Hong Kong, Tung Chee-hwa (China's choice to run Hong Kong after the British departure in 1997) to speak at one of the lunches. He spoke for the full time allotted, leaving none for questions, which prompted complaints from members such as Ruth Richardson that politicians should not generally be given a platform at the Society's meetings, and certainly not without facing questions. Her criticism was not lost on the meeting. But to other listeners, Tung's remarks came as a valuable but chilling warning about China's ambitions for Hong Kong and the South China Sea in general. It was also a stark reminder that China, though now an enormous trading nation, was by no means a benign and liberal free-market democracy, and that the free world's trade and other dealings with China should be tempered by that fact.

In Hong Kong, the new Secretary and Treasurer prompted the Board towards a reform agenda. Among the changes agreed were moving the *Newsletter* online, greater stringency on members in arrears, a more rules-driven membership process, more bursaries for young scholars and updating the Society's accounting technology. And there was talk of many other reforms. The retiring President, the American economist Allan Meltzer, summed things up with some trepidation: 'There's going to be changes. I don't know what they will be, but there will be changes.'

Constitutional changes

And changes there were. Running the Society had become a complex operation. It was now fifteen times larger than the original group who met in 1947. Its members were much more diverse in terms of age, gender and professional background. It had members on every continent. And like all such bodies, its operations were subject to the increasingly rigorous accounting and practice standards demanded by both the authorities and the professions. Clarke and Butler concluded that its constitution – drawn up in the 1960s – and the informality of the Society's procedures were no longer sufficient for the operation of what was now a large and prominent international organisation.

The four executive officers discussed the Society's organisational problems and agreed ways forward at a special meeting in London in February 2015. The legal corporation would be moved to Clarke's office in Chattanooga. A new website would be built, which would be designed to allow online processing of membership applications and secure credit card payments. New systems would be created to tighten internal accounting and ensure that accounts and legal documents were filed on time. The performance of the Society's investments would be reviewed. Any discrepancies found in the accounting numbers and the membership list would be worked through and resolved. The membership process would move to a more manageable annual cycle, fast-track membership would go, there would be firmer rules for members who were in arrears on their membership dues (now $100) and complimentary membership for the over-70s would be phased out. The Board would be slimmed down to twelve, there would be term limits on officers, expenses would be tightened and there would be written guidelines for Board and committee members. The Senate would be replaced with a Nomination Committee that would propose new Board appointments. To put all this into effect, the By-laws (the Society's constitution) would be redrafted by Butler and Clarke.

In 2016, the new rules were put to an online ballot of all 593 members in good standing and passed by an overwhelming majority. A motion to accept this result was put to the General Meeting in Miami and (although some past officers voiced strong concerns about the speed, nature and detail of the reforms) the changes were again accepted overwhelmingly.

More programme innovations

The 2016 meeting in Miami brought programme innovations too. Butler's survey of the members revealed that a sizeable number of them found the excursion, and the traditional opening dinner with an address by the President, too tiring – particularly when many had undertaken long and exhausting journeys just to get to the event in the first place. Miami therefore opened with an informal 'icebreaker' and members were given a choice of shorter excursions. Another innovation was poster sessions, allowing young scholars to present their research and discuss it with experienced members.

The innovations continued at the 2018 General Meeting in Gran Canaria. There were optional 10-minute 'Discovery Talks' on a variety of interests; group dialogues about important research papers; book presentations; an academic 'clinic' in which academics could help each other on their papers; a 'fireside chat' between PayPal co-founder Peter Thiel and science author Matt Ridley; artistic performances; and 'unconference' sessions enabling members to meet informally and discuss subjects of their choice. These new formats were given high approval ratings on the surveys filled out by the conference participants.

There were further developments at the 2020 Special Meeting held at the Hoover Institution in Palo Alto, California, with some of the set-piece lectures being filmed and the main papers being published in book form after the event. Anxious to preserve members' privacy in discussions, the Board insisted that the filming was preceded by an announcement that cameras were present and that they would be turned off before any discussion on the presenters' remarks, and presenters were asked for their permission to reproduce their papers before the book was assembled. Members and presenters seemed comfortable with these innovations.

Nevertheless, Linda Whetstone, who became President later that year, was keen to go further. She had long wanted to have the Society's papers, presentations and discussions recorded and made available online, for the benefit of people who were hungry for liberal ideas but could not afford to attend the Society's meetings – such as members of the many liberal activist groups in sub-Saharan Africa with whom she worked closely. There was some sympathy for this, though Whetstone's sudden death in 2021 robbed the idea of its most energetic advocate.

Even so, while the dissemination-versus-privacy tensions remain, it seems probable that, going forward, more and more of the Society's discussions will be made available to a wider public, enabling liberal activists from around the world to enjoy them and learn from them. Indeed, private recordings of some early meetings have come to light, opening up the prospect that future scholars will be able to listen to the spoken words of Hayek, Mises, Friedman and others from the Society's golden age.

The pandemic years

For many years, there has been a presumption that there are no other meetings in the (usually even-numbered) year of General Meetings. This is to prevent other meetings sapping support from what are the Society's flagship events, at which Board meetings, member meetings and elections are held. An exception was made with the 2020 Stanford meeting because of the high quality of the proposed agenda; but only after heated argument was a compromise decision reached to hold the event in January (a full eight months away from the planned 2020 General Meeting in Oslo), to designate it as a 'Special' meeting and to place a limit on the numbers attending.

As it turned out, Stanford would be the last meeting for 22 months. By April 2020, with the COVID-19 pandemic spreading, it had become clear that the Oslo meeting was no longer feasible. The organisers, Lars Peder Nordbakken and his colleagues at the think tank Civita, agreed to move the event to 2022, maintaining the cycle of even-year General Meetings and making it the 75th Anniversary meeting.

In the interim, the business of the Society carried on. Meetings of officers and of the Board were conducted online – not an easy task, given their spread across time zones. The election of Board members and officers was conducted by online ballot. There was talk of staging online conferences, though the idea found little favour. However, Gabriel Calzada of the Universidad Francisco Marroquín (UFM) proposed a physical meeting in Guatemala, marking UFM's fiftieth anniversary.

This meeting went ahead in November 2021. It too brought innovations, such as more of the spaces for mutual learning that Hayek had talked about, filming and posting online parts of the discussion, and a recap video made available to participants following the event. But the 2021 meeting had another significance too: it meant that the Society has held at least one meeting in every calendar year since 1969.

13 IMPACT, STRENGTHS AND CHALLENGES

The Society's contribution

Though liberal ideas today face many challenges, there seems no need for the Society to be pessimistic.

It is certainly true that illiberal governments rule over a large proportion of the world's population – China, Russia, parts of South East Asia, Africa, Latin America and elsewhere. Large world powers continue to bully their neighbours and large state institutions continue to bully ordinary citizens. Francis Fukuyama's liberal 'end of history' still seems a long way off.

Even supposedly liberal governments have proved reluctant to give up the powers they took on to fight Covid-19; 'cancel culture' threatens free speech, the discovery of truth and the development of ideas; the expansion of trade has enriched not merely individuals but repressive governments too, making them even more authoritarian at home and more assertive abroad. Then there remain questions of how – and even whether – liberal countries can stand up to those, at home and abroad, who would gladly extinguish liberal ideas and liberal society.

But it is equally true that the world's challenges seemed far graver to the small group of liberal thinkers who met at

Mont-Pèlerin in 1947; and yet, within half a century of that gathering, freedom was expanding into countries that were once bywords for oppression, state industries were being returned to the private sector, once closed-off regions of the globe were opening to investment and growth, and dollar-a-day poverty was giving way to prosperity and aspiration.

So there is every reason to believe that the Society's members today can rise to the present challenges and hope to overcome them. Indeed, their predecessors have left them a much firmer foundation on which to do so. The failure of central planning has been exposed, both intellectually and practically. Inflation is better understood than it once was. There is a widespread and healthy scepticism about the ability of governments to run almost anything efficiently, and a broader questioning about the motives of those in power. There is a greater appreciation of the value of peace and stability in a more interconnected world. Trade, in both goods and, increasingly, services has become not only global but also a familiar part of all of our lives. Militarism and aggression are much less respectable.

Moreover, markets have spread into areas once thought to be the preserve of the state. Margaret Thatcher, greatly influenced by Hayek and Friedman and supported by Society member Sir Geoffrey Howe, began Britain's privatisation of state industries, an idea that would go round the world, even into the former communist-led countries of Eastern Europe. Many other countries replaced their old state-run Ponzi-scheme pension systems with individuated private accounts like those designed by the Chilean minister (and Society member) José Piñera. School choice and school vouchers, ideas rediscovered and popularised by Friedman, began to reform and improve education in yet other places. Property rights have been expanded and business paperwork scaled back in large parts of South America, thanks to thinkers like the Peruvian economist (and another Society member) Hernando de Soto. And parts of the former Soviet bloc have opened up to (or returned to) social and economic freedom, thanks in large part to the ideas, understanding and influence of the Society members located there such as Mart Laar, Václav Klaus and Leszek Balcerowicz.

It is impossible to measure with any precision the impact of the Society in these achievements, and impossible to predict its influence on future events. In a very important sense, while its members may have considerable impact individually, the Society itself has none: it is, in Hayek's words, only a 'community of liberal scholars' with no policies or programme of its own. But by bringing authoritative liberal thinkers together, and by expanding the scope and depth of liberal ideas, it ensured that liberalism could not simply be ignored. By offering a challenging critique of socialist thinking, it guaranteed that the assumptions on which socialism was based, and the presumption of its beneficial results, could not simply be taken for granted. By providing its members with mutual support, it gave isolated liberals the strength to hold their ground against the seemingly overwhelming force of the political consensus. By creating networks of liberal scholarship, it brought liberal ideas to active and enquiring young minds across the world. By informing the work of liberal policy institutes and a few thinking politicians, it helped change real events. All these activities continue, and on an ever-expanding scale. So in that sense, the Society's influence will indeed continue to be significant.

Strength through diversity and debate

Like liberalism itself, the Society's membership has grown and spread. It started as a group of West Europeans and Americans, with some tensions between the two in terms of their analysis of the problems and their prescriptions for them.

Now there are large representations from Japan, Australasia, South America, Central America and Eastern Europe – and growing interest in Africa and the Middle East – but the tensions have gone. Certainly, there are still big differences in analyses and prescriptions. Yet the Society's members are easy in their international company, knowing that even in their differences they are all part of the same broad liberal approach. The Society strives to reflect this international and intellectual diversity in its Board and other management structures. All in all, the global spread of the Society, of liberal ideas, and of the freedom movement in general has never been wider. Even so, Society members remain keen to spread their ideas even more widely into more countries and into the thinking of more minds.

The diversity of the Society shows in other ways too. While members share a commitment to the free society and free economy, they embrace a wide range of views on what that means, as well as how to achieve it. They also come from a wide range of backgrounds. Although around half are academics, mostly economists, the Society benefits from having in its ranks many able and accomplished thinkers from business, think tanks, politics, journalism and public administration.

Like any association, the Society has its own internal critics. But as Hartwell points out, such criticism is always intended to improve how the Society works, not to challenge its fundamental purpose. Membership is seen as an honour, and the Society gives its members an enormous sense of belonging to something that is mutually supportive, stimulating and important.

The continuing challenge

Along with the political challenges, the intellectual challenges continue. As Feulner put it, 'Living in a society in which everyone "naturally" looks to government to solve every problem, how do we return power to the individual?' Making the welfare state societies of the West into free societies seems just as difficult as making the communist societies of the East into capitalist ones.

Added to which, there are new and more subtle problems about such transition processes themselves. Tyranny may be giving way to democracy in large parts of the world, but as Society members have explained, unlimited democratic power can threaten freedom by giving majorities the power to oppress and exploit minorities. Indeed, it is a common view that in many places, democracy has already elided into a baleful form of populism, with the public and politicians led along by the shrill demands of extreme and illiberal campaigners. If so, the question is what can liberals do about it?

Although more countries are experiencing freedom, freedom demands personal responsibility and brings moral dilemmas, as Hartwell observed. All these challenges also raise questions: how can we help people develop that necessary responsibility and how do we articulate the morality that allows human beings to live together in harmony?

At the 25th anniversary of the Society in 1972, some members argued that it had done its job and should be disbanded. But the job of defending liberty never ends. Each decade brings new challenges. As Hayek said when he founded the Society in 1947, working out a philosophy of freedom is a task that demands 'continuous effort'. Three-quarters of a century later, that effort still continues – informed and invigorated by the curious and intangible presence that is the Mont Pelerin Society.

FURTHER READING

Burgin, A. (2015) *The Great Persuasion: Reinventing Free Markets since the Depression*. Harvard University Press. (Traces the intellectual history of liberalism through bodies such as the Mont Pelerin Society, from a social philosophy with significant constraints on markets to the more thoroughgoing version of the 1960s and 1970s.)

Caldwell, B. (ed.) (2022) *Mont Pèlerin 1947: Transcripts of the Founding Meeting of the Mont Pèlerin Society* (foreword by John Taylor). Stanford, CA: Hoover Institution Press. (Well-researched account of the founding meeting by the Society's leading contemporary historian.)

Caldwell, B. and Klausinger, H. (2022) *Hayek: A Life, 1899–1950*. University of Chicago Press. (Informative intellectual biography of the Society's founder.)

Commun, P. and Kolev, S. (eds) (2018) *Wilhelm Röpke (1899–1966): A Liberal Political Economist and Conservative Social Philosopher*. Cham: Springer. (Intellectual biography of one of the Society's founder members and an architect of the German social market economy, designing the conditions that enabled the post-war economic miracle.)

Feulner, E. J. (1999) *Intellectual Pilgrims: The Fiftieth Anniversary of the Mont Pelerin Society*. Washington, DC: Heritage Foundation. (Short reflection on the Society's half-century, asking if liberalism has succeeded, outlining the principles of a free society and looking at how to renew social and economic freedom.)

Hartwell, R. M. (1995) *The History of the Mont Pelerin Society.* Indianapolis, IN: Liberty Fund Inc. (The definitive history of the Society's first four decades.)

Reinhoudt, J. and Audier, S. (2018) *The Walter Lippmann Colloquium. The Birth of Neo-Liberalism.* London: Palgrave Macmillan. (Account of the Paris meeting that inspired Hayek to draw liberals together again after the wartime intermission.)

White, L. H. (2012) *The Clash of Economic Ideas: The Great Policy Debates and Experiments of the Last Hundred Years.* New York: Cambridge University Press. (Masterly account of the history of economic debates and ideas in the twentieth century, tracing the journey from institutionalism to the revival of liberal ideas after 1947.)

PARTICIPANTS AT THE INAUGURAL MEETING IN 1947

Maurice Allais (1911–2010), École Nationale Supérieure des Mines, Paris, France. French economist and winner of the 1988 Nobel Prize in Economic Science for his work on market behaviour and efficient resource use.

Carlo Antoni (1896–1959), Istituto Nazionale per le Relazioni Cultural con l'Estro, Rome, Italy. Italian philosopher and historian, known for his work on historicism and his critique of German idealism, *The Revolt Against Reason.*

Hans Barth (1904-64), University of Zurich, Switzerland. Swiss journalist and philosopher, an editor of the *Neue Zürcher Zeitung* and later professor of philosophy, politics and ethics at Zurich University.

Karl Brandt (1899–1975), Stanford University, Palo Alto, California, US. German-born American agricultural economist.

Herbert C. Cornuelle (1920–1996), Foundation for Economic Education, New York, US [Observer]. American assistant to Leonard Read at the Foundation for Economic Education who later became a business leader and head of the Volker Fund.

John A. Davenport (1905–87), *Fortune Magazine*, New York, US. American journalist and editor, author of books on Churchill and on the US economy.

Stanley Dennison (1912–92), Gonville & Caius College, Cambridge, UK. British economist who opposed the ideas of J. M. Keynes.

Aaron Director (1901–2004), University of Chicago, US. Russian-born American economist who founded the *Journal of Law and Economics* in 1958.

Walter Eucken (1891–1950), University of Freiburg, West Germany. German economist, one of the developers of ordoliberalism and leading figure in the design of the German social market economy.

Erich Eyck (1878–1964), Oxford, UK. Exiled German-born jurist, political journalist and historian of Bismarck, the Weimar Republic, Pitt the Elder and William Gladstone.

Milton Friedman (1912–2006), University of Chicago, US. American monetary economist, author of *Capitalism and Freedom* and the TV series and book *Free to Choose*, awarded the Nobel Prize, 1976.

Harry D. Gideonse (1901–85), Brooklyn College, New York, US. Dutch-born US economist, President of Brooklyn College from 1939 to 1966 and Chairman of the civil rights think tank Freedom House.

Frank D. Graham (1890–1949), Princeton University, New Jersey, US. Canadian-born American Professor of International Finance, best known for his work on commodity reserve currencies and protectionism.

Floyd A. Harper (1905–73), Foundation for Economic Education, New York, US. American economist and writer, helped to create the Foundation for Economic Education, later founder of the Institute for Humane Studies.

Friedrich A. Hayek (1899–1992), London School of Economics and Political Science, London, UK. Austrian-born British economist and philosopher, author of *The Road to Serfdom* and *Constitution of Liberty*, awarded the Nobel Prize in 1974.

Henry Hazlitt (1894–1993), *Newsweek*, New York, US. American business journalist who also wrote for the *Wall Street Journal* and the *New York Times*, and author of *Economics in One Lesson*.

Trygve Hoff (1895–1982), Oslo, Norway. Norwegian editor of the *Farmand* business magazine, author of *Economic Calculation in the Socialist Society* (1938).

Albert Hunold (1889–1981), Fédération des Associations de Fabricants d'Horlogerie, Geneva, Switzerland. Swiss marketing executive and intellectual, author of books on employment, inflation, planning, the market economy and liberalism.

Bertrand de Jouvenel (1903–87), Paris, France. French philosopher and political economist, secretary to Czechoslovakia's first prime minister and author of *The Ethics of Redistribution*.

Carl Iversen (1899–1978), University of Copenhagen, Denmark. Danish economist best known for his work on international capital movements and growth without planning.

John Jewkes (1902–88), University of Manchester, UK. British professor of economic organisation, best known for his 1946 book *Ordeal by Planning* and work on the economics of innovation.

Frank H. Knight (1885–1972), University of Chicago, US. American economist and one of the founders of the Chicago School, known for his book on the role of the entrepreneur, *Risk, Uncertainty, and Profit.*

Henri de Lovinfosse (1897–1977), Waasmunster, Belgium [Observer]. Belgian engineering industrialist and entrepreneur, co-author (with French philosopher Gustave Thibon) of *Solución Sociale.*

Fritz Machlup (1902–83), University of Buffalo, US. Exiled Austrian-born US economist, one of the first economists to explore the role of knowledge as an economic resource.

Loren B. Miller (1906–58), Detroit Bureau of Governmental Research, Detroit, US. American civic reformer and libertarian activist who convinced many business leaders to support liberal and libertarian causes.

Ludwig von Mises (1881–1973), New York University, US. Austrian-born US economist and political scientist, and a leading figure in the socialist calculation debates, who developed the ideas of praxeology.

Felix M. Morley (1894–1982), Washington, DC, US. American journalist and editor, later Pulitzer Prize–winning editor at the *Washington Post* and Washington Editor of *Barron's Weekly.*

Michael Polanyi (1891–1976), University of Manchester, UK. Hungarian polymath who critiqued the Soviet planning of science and developed the theory of spontaneously organising polycentric orders.

Karl Popper (1902–94), London School of Economics and Political Science, London, UK. Austrian-born British philosopher noted for his work on the theory of knowledge, author of *The Open Society and Its Enemies* and later knighted.

William E. Rappard (1883–1958), Institut Universitaire des Hautes Études Internationales, Geneva, Switzerland. Swiss diplomat and economic historian who represented his country at the International Labour Organization and the United Nations.

Leonard E. Read (1898–1983), Foundation for Economic Education, New York, US. American co-founder of the Foundation for Economic Education and author of the essay *I, Pencil*, a fable on the division of labour.

George Révay (1921–2005), *Reader's Digest*, Paris, France [Observer]. Hungarian-born European Editor of *Reader's Digest* in Paris.

Lionel Robbins (1898–1984), London School of Economics and Political Science, London, UK. British economist and head of economics at the LSE who wrote on economic method and critiqued welfare economics; later became Lord Robbins.

Wilhelm Röpke (1899–1966), Institut Universitaire des Hautes Études Internationales, Geneva, Switzerland. Exiled German-born Swiss economist, one of the intellectual architects of the German social market economy that led to the country's post-war economic miracle.

George J. Stigler (1911–91), Brown University, Providence, US. American economist and key figure of the Chicago School, known for his work on regulatory capture and awarded the Nobel Prize in 1982.

Herbert Tingsten (1896–1973), University of Stockholm, Sweden. Swedish writer, newspaper publisher, political science professor and pioneer of election statistics.

François Trévoux (1900–89), University of Lyon, France. French law and economics professor who wrote on regulation but saw no clear line between the role of the state and of individuals.

V. Orval Watts (1889–1993), Foundation for Economic Education, New York, US. American economist, the first full-time economist in the Chambers of Commerce, who wrote on free enterprise and trade unionism.

Veronica Wedgwood (1910–97), *Time and Tide*, London, UK. British historian of the Thirty Years' War, the English Civil War, Richlieu, Charles I and Cromwell; made a Dame (DBE) in 1968

MEETINGS OF THE SOCIETY

1947   1st General Meeting, Mont-Pèlerin, Switzerland
1949   2nd General Meeting, Seelisberg, Switzerland
1950   3rd General Meeting, Bloemendaal, Holland
1951   4th General Meeting, Beauvallon, France
1953   5th General Meeting, Seelisberg, Switzerland
1954   6th General Meeting, Venice, Italy
1956   7th General Meeting, Berlin, Germany
1957   8th General Meeting, St Moritz, Switzerland
1958   9th General Meeting, Princeton, New Jersey, US
1959   10th General Meeting, Oxford, England
1960   11th General Meeting, Kassel, Germany
1961   12th General Meeting, Turin, Italy
1962   13th General Meeting, Knokke, Belgium
1964   14th General Meeting, Semmering, Austria
1965   15th General Meeting, Stresa, Italy
1966   Regional Meeting, Tokyo, Japan
1967   16th General Meeting, Vichy, France
1968   17th General Meeting, Aviemore, Scotland
1968   Regional Meeting, Caracas, Venezuela
1970   18th General Meeting, Munich, Germany
1971   Regional Meeting, Rockford, Illinois, US
1972   19th General Meeting, Montreux, Switzerland
         (25th Anniversary)
1973   Regional Meeting, Guatemala City, Guatemala

1973 Regional Meeting, Salzburg, Austria
1974 20th General Meeting, Brussels, Belgium
1975 Regional Meeting, Hillsdale, Michigan, US
1976 21st General Meeting, St Andrews, Scotland
1977 Regional Meeting, Amsterdam, Netherlands
1977 Regional Meeting, Paris, France
1978 22nd General Meeting, Hong Kong
1978 Special Meeting, Taipei, Taiwan
1979 Regional Meeting, Madrid, Spain
1980 23rd General Meeting, Stanford, California, US
1981 Regional Meeting, Viña del Mar, Chile
1981 Regional Meeting, Stockholm, Sweden
1982 24th General Meeting, Berlin, West Germany
1983 Regional Meeting, Vancouver, Canada
1984 25th General Meeting, Cambridge, England
1984 Regional Meeting, Paris, France
1985 Regional Meeting, Sydney, Australia
1986 26th General Meeting, St-Vincent, Italy
1987 Regional Meeting, Indianapolis, Indiana, US
1988 27th General Meeting, Tokyo and Kyoto, Japan
1988 Special Meeting, Taipei, Taiwan
1989 Regional Meeting, Christchurch, New Zealand
1990 28th General Meeting, Munich, West Germany
1990 Regional Meeting, Antigua, Guatemala
1991 Regional Meeting, Big Sky, Montana, US
1991 Regional Meeting, Prague, Czechoslovakia
1992 29th General Meeting, Vancouver, Canada
1993 Regional Meeting, Rio de Janeiro, Brazil
1994 30th General Meeting, Cannes, France
1995 Regional Meeting, Cape Town, South Africa

1996 31st General Meeting, Vienna, Austria

1996 Regional Meeting, Cancun, Mexico

1997 Special Meeting, Mont-Pèlerin, Switzerland
(50th Anniversary)

1997 Regional Meeting, Barcelona, Spain

1998 32nd General Meeting, Washington, DC, US

1999 Regional Meeting, Potsdam, Germany

1999 Regional Meeting, Vancouver, Canada

1999 Special Meeting, Bali, Indonesia

2000 33rd General Meeting, Santiago, Chile

2001 Regional Meeting, Bratislava, Slovakia

2002 34th General Meeting, London, England

2002 Special Meeting, Goa, India

2003 Regional Meeting, Chattanooga, Tennessee, US

2004 35th General Meeting, Salt Lake City, Utah

2004 Regional Meeting, Hamburg, Germany

2004 Special Meeting, Colombo/Kandalama, Sri Lanka

2005 Regional Meeting, Reykjavik, Iceland

2006 36th General Meeting, Guatemala City, Guatemala

2007 Special Meeting, Nairobi, Kenya

2008 37th General Meeting, Tokyo, Japan

2009 Regional Meeting, Stockholm, Sweden

2009 Special Meeting, New York City, New York, US

2010 38th General Meeting, Sydney, Australia

2010 Regional Meeting, Guatemala City, Guatemala

2011 Regional Meeting, Buenos Aires, Argentina

2011 Regional Meeting, Istanbul, Turkey

2011 Special Meeting, New Delhi, India

2012 39th General Meeting, Prague, Czech Republic

2012 Special Meeting, Fez, Morocco

2013 Regional Meeting, San Cristobel, Galapagos Islands

2014 40th General Meeting, Hong Kong

2015 Regional Meeting, Lima, Peru

2016 41st General Meeting, Miami, Florida, US

2017 Regional Meeting, Seoul, South Korea

2018 42nd General Meeting, Maspalomas, Gran Canaria

2019 Regional Meeting, Fort Worth, Texas, US

2020 Special Meeting, Stanford, California, US

2021 Special Meeting, Guatemala City, Guatemala

2022 43rd General Meeting, Oslo, Norway
      (75th Anniversary)

PRESIDENTS OF THE SOCIETY

Prof. Friedrich A. Hayek	UK	1947–61
Prof. Wilhelm Röpke	Switzerland	1961
Prof. John Jewkes	UK	1962–64
Prof. Friedrich Lutz	Germany	1964–67
Prof. Bruno Leoni	Italy	1967
Prof. Friedrich Lutz (interim President)		
	Germany	1967–68
Prof. Günter Schmölders	Germany	1968–70
Prof. Milton Friedman	US	1970–72
Prof. Arthur Shenfield	UK	1972–74
Prof. Gaston Leduc	France	1974–76
Prof. George J. Stigler	US	1976–78
Prof. Manuel Ayau	Guatemala	1978–80
Prof. Chiaki Nishiyama	Japan	1980–82
Lord Harris of High Cross	UK	1982–84
Prof. James M. Buchanan	US	1984–86
Prof. Herbert Giersch	Germany	1986–88
Prof. Antonio Martino	Italy	1988–90
Prof. Gary S. Becker	US	1990–92
Prof. Max Hartwell	UK	1992–94
Prof. Pascal Salin	France	1994–96
Dr Edwin J. Feulner Jr	US	1996–98
Dr Ramón Diaz	Uruguay	1998–2000
Prof. Christian Watrin	Germany	2000–2

Prof. Leonard P. Liggio	US	2002–4
Prof. Victoria Curzon–Price	Switzerland	2004–6
Greg Lindsay, AO	Australia	2006–8
Prof. Deepak Lal	US	2008–10
Prof. Kenneth Minogue	UK	2010–12
Prof. Allan H. Meltzer	US	2012–14
Prof. Pedro Schwartz	Spain	2014–16
Prof. Peter Boettke	US	2016–18
Prof. John B. Taylor	US	2018–20
Linda Whetstone	UK	2020–21
Prof. Gabriel Calzada (acting President)		
	Guatemala	2021–22

SECRETARIES

Albert Hunold	Switzerland	1948–60
Prof. Bruno Leoni	Italy	1960–67
Ralph Harris	UK	1967–76
Max Thurn	Austria	1976–88
Dr Carl-Johan Westholm	Sweden	1988–2010
Prof. Giancarlo Ibarguen	Guatemala	2010–12
Dr Eamonn Butler	UK	2012–20
Prof. Alberto Mingardi	Italy	2020–

TREASURERS

Prof. Charles O. Hardy	US	1948
Prof. W. Allen Wallis	US	1948–54
Prof. Fritz Machlup	US	1954–59
Prof. Clarence E. Philbrook	US	1959–69
Prof. Arthur Kemp	US	1969–79
Dr Edwin J. Feulner Jr	US	1979–2012
Prof. Jeff R. Clarke	US	2012–20
Prof. Benjamin Powell	US	2020–

NOBEL LAUREATES AMONG
MONT PELERIN SOCIETY MEMBERS

Prof. Friedrich A. Hayek	Economics	1974
Prof. Milton Friedman	Economics	1976
Prof. George J. Stigler	Economics	1982
Prof. James M. Buchanan	Economics	1986
Prof. Maurice Allais	Economics	1988
Prof. Ronald Coase	Economics	1991
Prof. Gary S. Becker	Economics	1992
Prof. Vernon L. Smith	Economics	2002
Prof. Mario Vargas Llosa	Literature	2010

ABOUT THE IEA

The Institute is a research and educational charity (No. CC 235 351), limited by guarantee. Its mission is to improve understanding of the fundamental institutions of a free society by analysing and expounding the role of markets in solving economic and social problems.

The IEA achieves its mission by:

- a high-quality publishing programme
- conferences, seminars, lectures and other events
- outreach to school and college students
- brokering media introductions and appearances

The IEA, which was established in 1955 by the late Sir Antony Fisher, is an educational charity, not a political organisation. It is independent of any political party or group and does not carry on activities intended to affect support for any political party or candidate in any election or referendum, or at any other time. It is financed by sales of publications, conference fees and voluntary donations.

In addition to its main series of publications, the IEA also publishes (jointly with the University of Buckingham), *Economic Affairs*.

The IEA is aided in its work by a distinguished international Academic Advisory Council and an eminent panel of Honorary Fellows. Together with other academics, they review prospective IEA publications, their comments being passed on anonymously to authors. All IEA papers are therefore subject to the same rigorous independent refereeing process as used by leading academic journals.

IEA publications enjoy widespread classroom use and course adoptions in schools and universities. They are also sold throughout the world and often translated/reprinted.

Since 1974 the IEA has helped to create a worldwide network of 100 similar institutions in over 70 countries. They are all independent but share the IEA's mission.

Views expressed in the IEA's publications are those of the authors, not those of the Institute (which has no corporate view), its Managing Trustees, Academic Advisory Council members or senior staff.

Members of the Institute's Academic Advisory Council, Honorary Fellows, Trustees and Staff are listed on the following page.

The Institute gratefully acknowledges financial support for its publications programme and other work from a generous benefaction by the late Professor Ronald Coase.

The Institute of Economic Affairs
2 Lord North Street, Westminster, London SW1P 3LB
Tel: 020 7799 8900
Fax: 020 7799 2137
Email: iea@iea.org.uk
Internet: iea.org.uk

Institute of
Economic Affairs

Raising the Roof: How to Solve the United Kingdom's Housing Crisis
Edited by Jacob Rees-Mogg and Radomir Tylecote
ISBN 978-0-255-36782-0; £12.50

How Many Light Bulbs Does It Take to Change the World?
Matt Ridley and Stephen Davies
ISBN 978-0-255-36785-1; £10.00

The Henry Fords of Healthcare … Lessons the West Can Learn from the East
Nima Sanandaji
ISBN 978-0-255-36788-2; £10.00

An Introduction to Entrepreneurship
Eamonn Butler
ISBN 978-0-255-36794-3; £12.50

An Introduction to Democracy
Eamonn Butler
ISBN 978-0-255-36797-4; £12.50

Having Your Say: Threats to Free Speech in the 21st Century
Edited by J. R. Shackleton
ISBN 978-0-255-36800-1; £17.50

The Sharing Economy: Its Pitfalls and Promises
Michael C. Munger
ISBN 978-0-255-36791-2; £12.50

An Introduction to Trade and Globalisation
Eamonn Butler
ISBN 978-0-255-36803-2; £12.50

Why Free Speech Matters
Jamie Whyte
ISBN 978-0-255-36806-3; £10.00

The People Paradox: Does the World Have Too Many or Too Few People?
Steven E. Landsburg and Stephen Davies
ISBN 978-0-255-36809-4; £10.00

An Introduction to Economic Inequality
Eamonn Butler
ISBN 978-0-255-36815-5; £10.00

Carbon Conundrum: How to Save Climate Change Policy from Government Failure
Philip Booth and Carlo Stagnaro
ISBN 978-0-255-36812-4; £12.50

Other IEA publications

Comprehensive information on other publications and the wider work of the IEA can be found at www.iea.org.uk. To order any publication please see below.

Personal customers

Orders from personal customers should be directed to the IEA:

IEA
2 Lord North Street
FREEPOST LON10168
London SW1P 3YZ
Tel: 020 7799 8911, Fax: 020 7799 2137
Email: sales@iea.org.uk

Trade customers

All orders from the book trade should be directed to the IEA's distributor:

NBN International (IEA Orders)
Orders Dept.
NBN International
10 Thornbury Road
Plymouth PL6 7PP
Tel: 01752 202301, Fax: 01752 202333
Email: orders@nbninternational.com

IEA subscriptions

The IEA also offers a subscription service to its publications. For a single annual payment (currently £42.00 in the UK), subscribers receive every monograph the IEA publishes. For more information please contact:

Subscriptions
IEA
2 Lord North Street
FREEPOST LON10168
London SW1P 3YZ
Tel: 020 7799 8911, Fax: 020 7799 2137
Email: accounts@iea.org.uk